D0875193

WITHDRAWN

Ezio d'Errico's
Theater of the Absurd

Ezio d'Errico's
Theater of the Absurd

THREE PLAYS

The Forest
The Siege
The Parkbench

Edited and with an Introduction
by Louis Kibler
Translated by Louis Kibler
and John Michael Stuart

Rutherford ● Madison ● Teaneck
Fairleigh Dickinson University Press
London and Toronto: Associated University Presses

Associated University Presses
440 Forsgate Drive
Cranbury, NJ 08512

Associated University Presses
25 Sicilian Avenue
London WC1A 2QH, England

Associated University Presses
P.O. Box 39, Clarkson Pstl. Stn.
Mississauga, Ontario
Canada L5J 3X9

The paper used in this publication meets the requirements
of the American National Standard for Permanence of Paper
for Printed Library Materials Z39.48-1984.

Library of Congress Cataloging-in-Publication Data

D'Errico, Ezio, 1892–1972.
  Ezio d'Errico's theater of the absurd : three plays / edited and
with an introduction by Louis Kibler ; translated by Louis Kibler
and John Michael Stuart.
    p.   cm.
  Includes bibliographical references.
  Contents: The forest — The siege — The parkbench.
  ISBN 0-8386-3399-4 (alk. paper)
  I. Kibler, Louis.   II. Stuart, John Michael.   III. Title.
PQ4813.R7A6   1991
852'.912—dc20   89-46417
                                                                  CIP

PRINTED IN THE UNITED STATES OF AMERICA

Contents

Acknowledgments

Without the financial support of a grant from Wayne State University's Faculty Research Award Program, it would have been impossible for me to undertake in Italy the research necessary for the present work.

I am deeply indebted to the Piccolo Teatro di Milano, whose archives provided an unexpected wealth of material on Ezio d'Errico. In particular I wish to thank the archivist Dr. Laura Guazzotti, whose professional expertise and many kindnesses not only greatly facilitated my work but also made my hours in the archives most pleasant.

To the heirs of the estate of Ezio d'Errico and especially to General Antonio d'Errico and to Ragioniere Silvio d'Errico, I am most grateful for their kind help and for their permission to translate into English the plays in this volume.

I am grateful to Harry Keyishian, Julien Yoseloff, Andrea Hammer, Michael Koy, and an unidentified reader for the excellent suggestions and help they gave during the editing phases of the manuscript.

Finally, I wish to thank my friend and collaborator, John Michael Stuart, for his fine translation of *La foresta;* I have made revisions to it, and I assume all responsibility for any inaccuracies or stylistic lapses.

LOUIS KIBLER

7

Ezio d'Errico's
Theater of the Absurd

\

Introduction

The British drama critic, Ossia Trilling, reviewing the 1958 world premiere of Ezio d'Errico's *Tempo di cavallette* (The year of the locusts), concluded his review by judging the play "brilliant and moving" and by advising his readers that "d'Errico is a name to remember."[1] Thirty years later, it is, unfortunately, a name recognized by few playgoers, even in the author's native Italy.

Despite a limited commercial and popular success of d'Errico's early preabsurdist plays written during 1948 to 1956, only one of his full-length and few of his avant-garde plays from the late fifties and early sixties were performed in Italy during his lifetime.[2] Productions were much more frequent elsewhere in Europe and in the Americas: his absurdist plays have been staged in translation in Germany, Switzerland, Austria, Hungary, and Argentina, and a one-act play, *Conversazione con Wladimiro* (Conversation with Vladimir) was performed in Italian by a Hunter College group in 1971. Still more works have been broadcast by the national radio networks of Switzerland, France, and Great Britain.

A recurring theme of Italian theater critics a quarter of a century ago is the shame that Italy should feel when one of her citizens is singled out for honors abroad and yet is almost totally ignored at home. Francesco Callari, for example, in his review of a series of three avant-garde plays given at the Volkstheater in Vienna in 1961 emphasized that d'Errico's *Tempo di cavallette* was received as warmly as Ionesco's *Tueur sans gages* (The killer) and Genet's *Le balcon* (The balcony). His conclusion, he says, can "only be bitter: we [Italians] have a dramatist who is esteemed and produced abroad on a level with Beckett, Ionesco, Adamov, Audiberti, Genet, Frisch, and others, but stubbornly ignored in Italy."[3] Taking a slightly different tack, Aldo Capasso also deplored the misfortune that confronted any dramatist born in Italy:

Our sincere admiration for the plays of Camus and Anouilh does not blind us to the fact that Italy has playwrights who are just as effective, touching, and representative of the anguish of our times. Had they had the good fortune to be born in France, they would have been nobly honored and brought to the attention of the world. Born in Italy, however, they can count on much less attention . . . and affection. . . . In this regard, the name that comes to mind first is that of Ezio d'Errico.[4]

The reasons for Italy's neglect of d'Errico were both economic and cultural. The Italian theater-going public of the fifties and sixties was not large, and the audience that was attracted to the experimental theater was even smaller, as it is in most countries. Almost any avant-garde production was predestined to lose money. Moreover, the preference of the Italian public tended toward light comedy; serious drama was attended well only if it had been canonized by the centuries (the works of Shakespeare, for example) or if it bore the cachet of the exotic or the universally approved (Brecht and Pirandello). Finally, Italy was still recovering from its age-old fascination with the *mattatore*, the star actor or actress whose virtuosity is almost an end in itself. The absurdist plays of Ezio d'Errico, however, are not star vehicles: the main characters in *L'assedio* (The siege), for example, are not clearly identifiable; Max and Margot are the principals in *La foresta* (The forest), yet neither is a protagonist in the usual sense of the word. No heroes in d'Errico's absurdist plays exist, but one could not find any meek or bumbling victims to call antiheroes, either. Such characters lying at the extremes of dramatic roles are markedly absent from the author's work. D'Errico's men and women are representative; they are the nonentities engendered by a depersonalized and mechanical universe, roles that scarcely show to best advantage the qualities of the star actor(s).

Although little place existed in Italy for d'Errico's absurdist dramas during his lifetime, it would appear that their fortunes have begun to rise slightly since his death in 1972. One of his finest works—*L'assedio*—was staged in the early seventies at Livorno. More recently and of still greater importance, the Il Pantano Company of Rome presented *Conversazione con Wladimiro, La sedia a dondolo* (The rocking chair), and *Il viaggio* (The trip) at the Teatro dell'Orologio. Under the direction of Claudio Frosi these one-act plays were also performed in March 1988 at the Palazzo dell'Ente Teatrale Italiano; the occasion was a conference organized by Maurizio Giammuso and devoted to d'Errico's work as a playwright of the absurd.

In addition to the support he has found among Italian critics, d'Errico's reception abroad has usually been favorable. Juan Guerrero Zamora praises *Tempo di cavallette* in the second volume of *Historia del teatro contemporaneo*.[5] Although Martin Esslin in his fundamental *The Theatre of the Absurd* limits himself to qualifying d'Errico as an "interesting Italian contribution to the Theatre of the Absurd," he speaks highly of *La foresta*.[6] The French playwright and novelist, Georges Sonnier, is more enthusiastic: after having read d'Errico's four full-length plays of the theater of the absurd, he writes that he is convinced that d'Errico's "dramatic universe is one of the most original and coherent of all contemporary theater. . . . Ezio d'Errico, in my opinion, has renewed all the old themes of tragedy, fusing them in a mold that conforms perfectly to our age of absurdity, anguish, and despair."[7]

* * *

Ezio d'Errico was born on 5 July 1892 in Agrigento, Sicily, not far from where Pirandello had been born twenty-five years earlier. Unlike the family of his fellow dramatist, however, d'Errico's parents were not of Sicilian origin: his mother was a Lombard and his father, a military officer temporarily stationed in Sicily, came from Puglia. Ezio, too, after studies at the famous Nunziatella Military Academy in Naples, began a career in the armed forces. He became an officer in the highly respected Bersaglieri corps and served during World War I; by the late 1920s he had risen to the rank of lieutenant colonel. Then, eligible for a military pension, the thirty-six-year-old d'Errico resigned his commission and began the first of many career changes.

While still in the service, he had worked in various plastic media; when he left it, he went to Paris to study painting, supplementing his income by working as an engraver, ceramist, and photographer. Returning to Italy in 1930, he lived in Milan where he affiliated himself with the leading Italian avant-garde painters—Lucio Fontana, Osvaldo Licini, Virginio Ghiringhelli, Mauro Reggiani, and Atanasio Soldati. Indeed, he joined with them in the epochal abstractionist exhibition—the first in Italy—at Turin in 1935. The plastic arts were for d'Errico a lifelong passion: he had more than sixty collective and personal exhibitions, the last one taking place in May 1970 at the Galleria Levi in Rome.

In the mid-1930s d'Errico moved to Turin; there he began his literary career by assuming the editorship of *Graphicus,* a review devoted to the arts. It is also about this time that he began to write creatively, first preparing radio scripts and in 1937 publishing a collection of short stories, *Parabole 1937* (Parables 1937).[8] Many of the twenty-five Kafkaesque, almost surrealist stories in this collection presage d'Errico's later theater of the absurd; an aura of poetry pervades the dreamlike atmosphere in which the characters exist and attempt to establish an identity. Often narrated in a strangely disembodied first person, the stories are rarely situated in identifiable geographic locations, nor does the reader often learn the given names of the characters. In Mussolini's Italy, so nationalistic and inimical to any form that could not be integrated into Italian tradition, *Parabole* and a later volume, *Da liberati* (As free men),[9] passed almost unnoticed. Success and renown would have to come to d'Errico from some quarter other than his avant-garde painting and writing. And it did.

In 1938 the Milanese publishing house of Mondadori launched d'Errico as a mystery writer, and the score of detective novels that he wrote in the following years established the former army officer as the Italian counterpart to Georges Simenon. His success in Italy was such that it earned him, as one critic maintained, the title of creator of the detective novel "all'italiana."[10] In the postwar period, d'Errico continued his activity in the field of fictional criminology by founding and directing for seven years the successful weekly magazine *Crimen*.

A "rabid anti-Fascist,"[11] d'Errico spent the war years in Rome, where he engaged in clandestine activities against the regime. *Noi due disarmati* (Both of us disarmed)[12] is a series of the author's recollections of his life with his dog during the war. After the fall of Fascism, he founded and directed during the years 1944 to 1945 a political newsweekly, *Folla*.

Having already contributed significantly to popular literature with his crime novels, d'Errico was to make one more important contribution to this field. In 1948 he created for the weekly magazine *Sogno* a new genre, the *fotoromanzo*, which has maintained a consistently high level of popularity in Italy for the past forty years. The *fotoromanzo* is a story—almost always a love story—told with pictures and words encapsulated in "balloons," like the American comic book. The illustrations, however, are not drawn but are instead photographs of live models. The heroine of d'Errico's first *fotoromanzo* was an aspiring young actress named Gina Lollobrigida.[13]

For our interests, however, 1948 is significant for a different reason: it is the year in which d'Errico, already in his midfifties, submitted a play, *Un uomo in più* (One man too many), to the jury of the Concorso Scuola del Teatro Drammatico, a theatrical competition. *Uomo* won first place, and it was staged in November of that year in Milan in the Teatro Sant'Erasmo. In the following twenty years d'Errico would devote much of his time to the theater, writing nearly forty plays, not counting many scripts for radio, television, and the cinema. In 1952 he began to write for the theatrical review *Ridotto* a monthly column that he continued until his death in Rome on 20 April 1972.

*　*　*

Most of d'Errico's early plays are of little interest today, though they were moderately successful with the public and with critics in the fifties. *Incontro coi superstiti* (Encounter with the survivors) won Palermo's Luigi Pirandello Prize in 1953 and *Le forze* (The powers) was awarded the Naples Prize of 1957. *La sei giorni (The Six Day Race)* is probably d'Errico's best-known play of this period. Chosen from 162 entries, it received the 1953 Istituto del Dramma Italiano-Piccolo Teatro Prize, the merit of which can be judged by the quality of the eight jurors, among whom were Mario Apollonio, Silvio D'Amico, Achille Fiocco—leading Italian scholars of the theater—and Eugenio Montale, the Nobel Prize winner who is regarded as the most important poet of twentieth-century Italy. Produced by the prestigious Piccolo Teatro di Milano and directed by Giorgio Strehler, *La sei giorni* premiered on 18 December 1953 and closed a week later after nine performances. Critical reaction to the work was mixed: the Communist newspaper *Unità* thought that it was "cold and arid," and the popular weekly *Oggi* found it disgusting; favorable notices, however, appeared in Milan's highly respected *Corriere della Sera* and the Florentine periodical *Realismo Lirico*.[14] The majority of reviews fell between these extremes, with most critics judging the theatrical production superior to the script.

Of d'Errico's preabsurdist period (i.e., before 1956), the most interesting play is also his first public success, *L'oggetto* (The object), which placed second in the Concorso Riccione in 1949 and which, under the direction of the brilliant Luigi Squarzina, premiered at Rome's Teatro Ateneo on 13 April 1950. *L'oggetto* distinguishes itself from d'Errico's other plays of the period by the antitraditional character of many of its elements, which prefigure the plays of his theater of the absurd later in the decade. In *L'oggetto*, d'Errico intentionally reduced the plot to an almost barren simplicity. The protagonist, Carlo, is in a state of depression; life in general is prosaic and disgusting, but in particular Carlo is unhappy with his wife. A friend tells him that certain objects have a mysterious power, and at the end of the first act a deaf-mute gives Carlo a brass object. Almost immediately the world of Carlo brightens; his wife announces that she is leaving, and Carlo wins a court action in which he is awarded 300,000 lire. As a protest against all of his previous life and as an unselfish blow for innocence and beauty, he gives the money to his niece, Irene, to publish her poetry. Overly confident, Carlo convinces himself that it is he alone who has changed his fortune, and he throws the object into the garbage. Almost immediately his world changes; the decision in his lawsuit is appealed and reversed, and Irene interprets his unselfish gift as an attempt to seduce her. Worse, she confesses to Carlo that she is a whore. Disillusioned and more desperate than ever, Carlo suddenly remembers the object and begins to look for it in the garbage heap. His rummaging about raises a cloud of dust and, to slake his thirst, he drinks by mistake muriatic acid and dies. His housemaid attempts to put flowers on his corpse, but Irene maintains that it is more appropriate for human beings to be buried beneath garbage.

Although such grotesque and cynical plays were rare on Italian stages at midcentury, even more original were the unconventional stage techniques. Because no doors or other exits led offstage, all the players were always onstage; called "transparent characters" by d'Errico, those who had finished their stage action would move to the side, sit down, and stare at the ground. Not only were there dialogues between characters, but the characters also talked to themselves and to their phantasms. This latter technique recurs in *La foresta*, when the Boy speaks with the saxophone. Finally, d'Errico urged that the costuming and makeup be "picturesque"; Irene, for example, a poor but imaginative young girl, wears a hat composed of three dried leaves.

"Because of the incontrovertible validity of its content and because of its technical innovations, *L'oggetto* is a work to be regarded as a positive contribution to the contemporary Italian theater." Thus wrote Leonida Rèpaci soon after *L'oggetto* opened in Rome. "The work," judged Rèpaci, "is moving in a certain direction, the right one, I think."[15] With the illumination of hindsight, it is now certain in which direction d'Errico was moving in April 1950, one month before Ionesco's *La cantatrice chauve* (The bald soprano) opened in Paris; it was toward what would later be known as the theater of the absurd. Still, another five years would pass before d'Errico would fulfill the promise of *L'oggetto* and write a play clearly in the mode of Ionesco and Beckett.

Although d'Errico's life was characterized by abrupt shifts in career, his decision to discard on the threshold of old age a reasonably successful theatrical career in favor of a new and untried genre requires explanation. The author himself offers a plausible one, and, what is even more important, provides an insight into his character and his attitude toward art.

> I began writing for the Theater when my hair was already gray; between 1948 and 1956 I had a score of plays produced, two or three new ones every year. But one day I asked myself if it was worthwhile continuing along this road that had become almost too easy and my conscience, which had perhaps been lying in wait for me at this crossing, replied: "no." I even became ashamed of having had so many plays staged (incidentally, let me say that the best ones, though they won national competitions, never made it to the stage); I concluded that, having now learned perfectly well how to build a "well-made scene" and how to obtain certain "effects," I had reached the point where it was time to throw everything out and begin all over again. There was nothing heroic in this decision. I had simply opened my eyes and realized that my infatuation was misplaced. It was somewhat like realizing that you had been in love with a woman who wasn't worth it. And so I destroyed all my experience, I threw the old tricks into the sea, made a clean slate of stage conventions, knocked the "character" from his altar, and I started over from the beginning. Today, no one in Italy asks me for a play. That gives me hope that I have taken the right road. The road of unpopularity.[16]

Like his earlier works, d'Errico's theater of the absurd is, to a certain extent, eclectic. The themes of sequestration and the need for the judgment of others recall some of Jean-Paul Sartre's plays. D'Errico is also heavily indebted to Ugo Betti, with whom he shares a concern for moral problems and from whom he has borrowed certain metaphors, specifically that of the *ingranaggio*, the machine whose mesh of gears ensnares men without hope of escape. His best full-length plays, *La foresta*, written in 1956, and *L'assedio*, in 1959, resemble the works of Samuel Beckett insofar as they present alienated people in a setting that is not readily identifiable with any particular society or geographic location. In these plays, the stage becomes a metaphysical place where the characters act out their drama—and ours.

In other ways, d'Errico's theater is quite different from Beckett's; if the Italian playwright's social and geographic settings are often vague, no doubt exists that we are in the twentieth century. World War II, anti-Semitism, the atomic bomb, and the wars in Southeast Asia all figure conspicuously in his plays. Moreover, Beckett's creatures are static, they seem to be suspended in an eternal present. The characters of d'Errico evolve; each of them has a coherent history and a conception of his destiny. Finally, Beckett presents the absurdity of the world as an absolute, as though it has always existed and to the same degree that it is now experienced by his characters. For d'Errico, absurdity is an evolutionary process, and he probes its causes while he projects its future.

Martin Esslin's classification of the various kinds of theater of the absurd can clarify d'Errico's position within it. The critic accepts Ionesco's definition of the absurd: "'Absurd is that which is devoid of purpose. . . . Cut off from his religious, metaphysical, and transcendental roots, man is lost; all his actions become senseless, absurd, useless.'"[17] Esslin then goes on to describe three distinct ways of treating the theme of the absurd. The first is that of the Existentialist theater of Sartre, Camus, Anouilh, and others, who present the new idea of absurdity within the old framework of the conventional theater; here the theme is argued logically and lucidly (i.e., a rational discussion of the irrational). The theater of the absurd, on the contrary, strives to give a new form to the new content; it attempts to present the absurd as it is experienced rather than arguing about it in a rational way. Indeed, rational discourse undergoes a radical devaluation among the playwrights of the theater of the absurd, which separates them from a third distinct but similar band of dramatists that includes Michel de Ghelderode, Jacques Audiberti, Georges Neveux, Georges Schéhadé, Henri Pichette, and Jean Vauthier. Esslin calls these writers the "poetic avant-garde."

> The "poetic avant-garde" relies on fantasy and dream reality as much as the Theatre of the Absurd does; it also disregards such traditional axioms as that of the basic unity and consistency of each character or the need for a plot. Yet basically the "poetic avant-garde" represents a different mood; it is more lyrical, and far less violent and grotesque. Even more important is its different attitude toward language: the "poetic avant-garde" relies to a far greater extent on consciously "poetic" speech; it aspires to plays that are in effect poems, images composed of a rich web of verbal associations.[18]

Ezio d'Errico's position in the theater lies somewhere between the theater of the absurd and the poetic avant-garde. Esslin has noted, for example, that "d'Errico's dream world, absurd and harsh though it may be, has a wistful poetic symbolism."[19] The most telling difference and similarity between d'Errico's use of language and that of the Francophone absurdists, however, is revealed in a comparison of the final scene of his *Il formicaio* (The ant heap) with that of Ionesco's *Les chaises* (The chairs).

In the latter play, the Orator finally appears to pronounce the message that has been prepared by the Old Man during his ninety-five years and that, he believes, will assure his eternal fame. When the Orator opens his mouth to speak, however, there issue forth only nonsense words, the unintelligible mutterings of a deaf-mute: "He, Mme, mm, mm. / Ju, gou, hou, hou. / Heu, heu, gu, gou, gueue."[20] It is a cruel joke perpetrated on an old man who has just committed suicide and on an unwary and unsuspecting public, which had expected significant words (perhaps those that would explain the play!) and was treated instead to mutterings devoid of any sense whatsoever, absurd words indeed.

D'Errico's *Il formicaio* also ends with a speech consisting of apparently meaningless words; Casimiro, the protagonist of the play, mounts a table and intones a long harangue to the assembled townspeople: "To-to . . . Torototò . . . To-to . . . Ta-tò . . . Ta-tò . . . Ta-tò."[21] Although these words are in appearance nonsense syllables quite like those uttered by Ionesco's Orator, they are in effect very different from them. The words themselves may lack a semantic function, but they nevertheless convey meaning when one considers their context, the tone in which they are spoken, and the interpretation given to them by many of the other characters in the play. The Knifegrinder has noted earlier in the play that all public speeches of a political or bureaucratic nature are similar; they are, he says, a sequence of "To-tò . . . Torototò" (226). Thus, Casimiro's pronouncing such a speech at the end of *Il formicaio* represents in part the abandonment of his freedom and individuality for the conformity of a mechanical and repressive society. Then, too, the tones in which the words are pronounced mimic those of the usual orator: accompanied by Casimiro's gestures, the tone, as indicated by the stage directions, is by turns emphatic, conciliatory, sad, energetic, interrogative, caricatural, good-humored, peremptory, imploring, annoyed, negative, ironic, and resigned. The playgoer perceives a series of attitudes on the part of the speaker that can be likened to the attitudes of speakers in "real" life. This contrast between the absurd and the real, what Henri Bergson would call the mechanical plastered onto the living,[22] affords some moments of humor for the audience; at the same time, the tones and gestures convey general emotional states. We are no longer in the realm of total and absolute absurdity. In fact, most of the onstage characters who are listening to Casimiro seem to understand what he is saying. Their comments and their repetition of Casimiro's meaning are germane to the principal themes of the play, as we shall see later. In short, the absurd features of his theater are never far from the reality of what d'Errico perceives as an irrational and alienated society.

Both eclectic and original, d'Errico eludes classification within traditional categories. The playwright himself, to my knowledge, never called himself either "absurdist" or "avant-garde"; he found the latter term particularly abhorrent,[23] even though one must agree with Giorgio Prosperi, who, after noting that d'Errico was one of the best-known members of the Italian avant-garde, maintains that his "true vocation was his taste for experimentation, his wanderings in reality and in the imagination."[24] As for other critics, they applied several different terms to d'Errico's work. Certain German critics defined d'Errico's new theater as "analogical," because it "progressed by means of analogies, symbols, *états d'âme*, resemblances among distinct things and persons and facts."[25] Georges Sonnier termed d'Errico's a "theater of solitude,"[26] whereas the esteemed historian of the Italian theater, Mario Apollonio, spoke of "antifigurative abstractionism."[27] It should be apparent that any attempt to pigeonhole d'Errico is likely to meet with failure or at least incompleteness. The judgment that Aldo Capasso, one of the best informed of d'Errico's critics, has passed on the writer and his work seems to me among the most accurate:

> D'Errico is fundamentally and very sincerely, warmly, and effectively, an anarchist who places no faith in the orthodox and moderate thinker, rejects the verdicts of courts (which are of necessity always summary and simplistic), disdains the facile classifications of current morality, and never forgets that there are two sides to every truth and at least two sides to every person. His works, which are totally expressive, totally beautiful, have all . . . been inspired by his revolt—not devoid of the tragic—against the simplistic unilaterality of orthodox judgments.[28]

* * *

Although d'Errico wrote little about his own works, his idea of a theater can be synthesized from a series of essays and interviews in the early sixties, most of which appeared in the monthly review *Il Dramma*. In them the dramatist revealed what he regarded as deficiencies in the contemporary theater, and he proposed a new theater that would be more consonant with the roles of modern men and women in the world.

D'Errico in his essays is pitiless toward the theater as it then existed in Italy. He favors the abolition of traditional plot and character. The latter element includes doing away with the *mattatore* (star system), and it involves the disappearance or at least the diminution of the concept of the character as an individual with a unique personality; this will be replaced by the dramatic "type." He also calls for the destruction of the so-called realist theater, "that bureaucratic image of reality which for centuries has been imposed on us by a traditionalist culture, a Theater that is all false, not a falseness that appears to be true but a falseness that is absolutely false."[29]

Other kinds of theater fare no better beneath d'Errico's pen. The "théâtre à thèse," for example, evokes his wrath, and he calls for the abolition of "the investigative theater, the political theater, the tribunal theater, because Art is not sociology, it is not a religious sermon, it is not supposed to correct morals and manners or to educate; it is simply supposed to be Art."[30] Using Umberto Eco's important critical study, *Opera aperta* (The open work),[31] as a point of departure, d'Errico inveighs against the "closed work of art, which embraces only one meaning—that of its author."[32] In its place he proposes the "open" theater:

> In my view "open" theatrical works break with the techniques used in the classical theater (by devaluing the plot, by abolishing the "mattatore" protagonist and the "big scene," etc.) and seek a new perspective by means of an analogical language and a stimulating dialogue. Such techniques will lead to a provocative situation that will oblige the spectator to enter into the debate in order to discover, among the many possible solutions, the one that he decides is best. I am advocating a theater in which the author himself will have no more authority than does the public in regard to the meaning of what he has written. The author thus becomes a "mediator" who instead of imposing his messages (as in the "théâtre à thèse") limits himself to transmitting revelations on the characters who have "invaded" him.
>
> At this point I expect objections from all those who maintain that the author must be superior to his work; but I regard him as the instrument of obscure forces within himself, and only these forces have the power, in a propitious moment of rapture, to burst forth and consolidate themselves into a synthesis. This synthesis is in part unconscious; the only thing the artisan remains aware of is that small part of his creativity which permits him to clothe his creations and render them perceptible to the spectator in a theatrically effective way.[33]

In the place of the traditional analytic and psychological drama
that purports to plumb the innermost reaches of the individual's
psyche, d'Errico, almost echoing some of the tenets of Marinetti's
Futurist Theater, proposes a theater of synthesis:

> Art is synthesis . . . and in a certain sense it cannot have a beginning
> and an end; instead, it should represent "an instant in motion." It
> must be a theater that has its own language and that offers only
> scattered analogies with certain real situations; it interprets selected
> states of the psyche by displacing the perspective in order to convey
> meanings that are nonetheless only emblematic.[34]

In response to a survey on the theater, the dramatist elaborated on
his vision of a theater of synthesis:

> Instead of representing on the stage the unhappiness, the aspirations,
> the hopes, and the anguish of humanity, we must undertake to "sum-
> marize" them in a dramatic synthesis in which there will still be a place
> for a certain plot and a certain typing of characters; but these must
> never overshadow the poetic mystery nor detract from a certain
> language that seeks new "depths."[35]

D'Errico explains and in a way justifies his untraditional theatrical
techniques on the grounds that a new kind of civilization demands
a new kind of theater:

> We are on the threshold of a cosmic era that will have unforeseeable
> effects on humanity; it is possible that the discoveries of tomorrow will
> force us to revise our philosophical systems and to modify our social
> structures. In the theater, too, we are trying to prepare for this future
> (which is already upon us in the form of a spiritual deepening and
> elevation) by seeking new ways of mythicizing, with a new poetics, the
> coarse drudgery of daily life, the unquenchable yearning of the man
> who knocks on the door of the unknown to seek an answer to his
> anguished questions.[36]

For d'Errico this new theater that will be consonant with the
contemporary world and especially with his brave new world of
the future is properly the theater of the absurd. It alone has
achieved the synthesis that d'Errico advocates. Equally important
to d'Errico, for whom the world is fundamentally an unresolvable
and unexplainable contradiction, the theater of the absurd can
accommodate and indeed thrive on contradiction. It is a theater
that is "bitter when it is comic, and grotesque when it is dramatic";[37] the comic and dramatic themselves coexist in it. The

theater of the absurd, he writes, is "philosophical without espousing Philosophy, it is poetic without invoking Literature . . . and it has no relation with the phenomenal reality that surrounds us. . . . The Theater of the Absurd has finally broken a tradition and has *gone beyond*. It has abandoned definitively the 'provincial' for the 'universal.' "[38]

* * *

D'Errico wrote his most original and effective absurdist dramas during the brief period from 1956 to 1959. Although he wrote several plays during the sixties, most were short works in one act, and their form and even content were almost as close to his traditional plays of the late forties and early fifties as they were to plays like *La foresta* or *L'assedio*. The full-length *Qualcuno al cancello* (Someone at the gate, 1960), for example, is more reminiscent of Betti than of Beckett. Although the setting and violent ending of *La panchina* (The parkbench) strongly recall Edward Albee's *The Zoo Story*, the Italian play certainly does not constitute an evolution in the development of d'Errico's absurdist vein. Other plays are even less daring: *Incontro col gentleman* (Encounter with a gentleman) is the tale of a meeting with Jack the Ripper in nineteenth-century London, *La visita* (The examination) concerns a postwar encounter between a sadistic concentration camp doctor and one of his former victims, and *Conversazione con Wladimiro* is little better than a television drama. In sum, d'Errico's reputation as a serious and important practitioner of the theater of the absurd resides in the four full-length plays that he wrote during the last half of the decade of the fifties.

Tempo di cavallette is d'Errico's first full-length play in the line of the theater of the absurd. Written in 1956, it reached the stage first in German translation *(Die Heuschrecken)* at Darmstadt on 6 March 1958. Subsequent productions appeared in Lucerne and Buenos Aires (1959) and in Vienna (1961). In the latter city, *Tempo* was presented as part of a series of three avant-garde works, the other two being Ionesco's *Tueur sans gages* and Genet's *Le balcon*. Aside from the prestige lent to it by sharing the billing with two of France's most important playwrights, *Tempo* enjoyed a generally favorable reception by critics. Italo Alighiero Chiusano called it "the only significant attempt made by an Italian . . . to insert our theater into the most vital current of the European avant-garde theater,"[39] and Ossia Trilling regarded the work as "a tract for the times."[40]

In *Tempo di cavallette* Joe, an Italian-American, returns to Italy to realize the dream that he has carried within himself for many years. After a lifetime of hard work and self-denial, he has amassed enough wealth to live comfortably in the land of his ancestors. Joe is forthright and guileless; he wants only order, peace, and the opportunity to establish a family by marrying an impoverished baroness with whom he has corresponded for several years. Joe is on his way to meet her at last when he stops in a small village to have his Cadillac checked by a mechanic.

In an act of generosity that astounds a young couple, Mattia and Giunchiglia, Joe lets them take a pleasure drive in his automobile. Mattia searches the car for clues to its owner's identity and discovers a box full of money. At the end of the first act, Mattia cruelly murders Joe in the presence of Giunchiglia, and, after hiding the body, they flee the village. The second act takes place three months later. The Baroness and her lawyer arrive in the village to seek news of Joe. Although she still loves him, she is convinced that he is dead and now needs proof of it to claim the legacy he has willed to her. The villagers deny that anyone named Joe has ever been in their town, but soon she hears the sound of his guitar and claims to see Joe—or at least his spirit. Joe eventually manifests himself in such a way that he can be seen by everyone except Giunchiglia and Mattia, who has returned impenitent from the foreign legion. The problem of crime and punishment is resolved when a mysterious white ash begins falling from the sky and kills everyone present except a small boy.

In its broad outlines, *Tempo* is almost a morality play: the innocent wayfarer is murdered with the connivance of an entire village that is eventually punished for its violation of the laws of hospitality. It is much more, however. D'Errico subtitles it a "tragic farce"; in addition, it is a satire of Italian civilization.

The setting of the play is amid the ruins of a bombed-out village. Joe thinks at first that the devastation was caused by World War II, but his mistaken assumption is corrected by the villagers, who explain that the government had declared their town a depressed area and destroyed it with the intention of constructing higher up the mountain a modern town with schools, hospitals, electricity, and safe water. To this end taxes were raised, loans arranged, laws proposed. New land has already been allotted to the residents, and as soon as the new laws have been approved by the Committee on Subcommittees and by the two houses of Parliament, then bids will be let out and work will begin. It is not certain, however, that the villagers will want to live in the new town, for old habits are tenacious. As the Hunter, who serves as the play's philosopher, remarks: "The government can't change men; no government has ever been able to do that—at least, not in Italy" (21).

The peninsula is, according to d'Errico, a tragic land, a land of volcanoes and earthquakes and floods. Its ponderous bureaucracy compounds disaster, whereas the character of its people is a major obstacle to achieving a modern, free state. The Italians' preoccupation with their common Roman heritage distracts them from contemporary concerns, yet it does little to neutralize their propensity for civil war. They are a people of contradictions ("No Italian is ever what he seems to be," states the Photographer [46]) who vaunt their individualism but cannot resist joining a religious procession or a political or military parade where they relinquish to the leader of the group their right to think independently. Now, the gap between the old and new generations is creating an even more unlivable world. Unlike their forebears, Giunchiglia and Mattia are strangers to affection, respect for their elders, and a sense of community. Theirs is a world in which only two values—materialism and rock 'n' roll music—exist.

Although a satiric-humorous vein runs throughout d'Errico's theater of the absurd, none of his other plays deals so precisely and thoroughly with the problems of Italy. Indeed, this aspect of *Tempo* is not absurdist at all but rather has its roots in the eighteenth-century social comedies of Carlo Goldoni. We must look elsewhere in the play for d'Errico's originality and for those elements that are characteristic of his theater of the absurd.

Few of the characters who people his play are well rounded. D'Errico shows little interest in the psychology of the individual; rather, his creations are generic, they are types embodying certain attitudes, and as such they are most often identified by their professions or social position. Thus, most bear no Christian or family name but are known as "The Hunter," "The Lawyer," "The Baroness," "The Gravedigger." Similarly, the author sometimes suggests in the scenic directions that the characters should move in such a way as to give the impression of marionettes, which further contributes to their depersonalization.

Within certain limits, one might characterize d'Errico's theater as a theater of absence. Not only are props not abundant, but their lack is notable. The Hunter, for example, does not carry a gun, and his cartridge belt is empty; the Photographer has no camera—he lost it during one of the frequent natural cataclysms. In compensation, he has become, in his words, an artist-pho-

tographer, shooting psychological portraits of his subjects. Inter-
locutors, too, are often absent. Serafina addresses her dead sons,
and the Accountant opens the play by justifying himself to his
superior, who is not on stage.

Tempo also introduces one of the principal metaphors of d'Errico's theater of the absurd—the train as a symbol of death. Other
trains of similar significance will reappear in *La foresta* and *La
panchina,* but nowhere is the absurdity of unexpected death more
clearly depicted than in *Tempo.* Joe muses over the capriciousness
of God's selecting those who are to die:

> No one knows how much time is left. Only God knows, and we cannot
> understand; we are on a train that runs along swiftly, and then—
> suddenly—God makes a sign and says, "That one, over there . . . yes,
> that one over there who is crying because he is unhappy . . . throw him
> off the train"; then death, who is the conductor, stops the train and
> the passenger gets off. His trip is over . . . Or else God makes a sign
> and says, "No, no, the other one; the one who is laughing because he is
> so happy" . . . The conductor stops the train and the one who was
> happy gets off. [*With a sigh.*] We cannot understand! (26)

It is in the realm of d'Errico's ideas and his conception of the
contemporary world, however, that *Tempo* is most profoundly
characteristic of d'Errico's theater of the absurd. It seems to be the
fount from which most of his other works spring. Here, for
example, in Serafina's mourning for her martyred sons, we find
the author's outrage at the futility of war: shortly before their
execution the three young men had written that they were facing
death serenely, with the certain knowledge that their deaths were
necessary to bring about a new world. "But where is that new
world?" Serafina implores. Where indeed? The Clerk says that
even as a boy he heard people talking about a new world: "When
the Great War broke out, everyone said it would be the last one
and that a new world would arise from it . . . Wrong . . . They
were deceived. People continued to talk about war, and they
talked so much that it wasn't long before a new war broke out,
more catastrophic than the first one" (18–19). The new world is
always just out of grasp, for without freedom no new world can
exist. Government leaders—whatever their politics—always place
a higher priority on order than on freedom, however. Governments may rise and fall, but the old world remains with us,
explains the Lawyer, who voices d'Errico's pessimism and thinly
veiled anarchism:

All regimes are police states, everywhere in the world. . . . Regimes change, but it is always the same men who hold power. Only their clothing is different. In countries where the rulers have worn uniforms for too long, a revolution occurs and jackets and turtleneck sweaters triumph. When the jackets and sweaters have ruled too long, there is a revolution and sabers and boots come to power. (56)

Justice and humane governments do not exist in d'Errico's world. On the contrary, government is a machine that ensnares the helpless. Nor is life itself very different. It is perhaps best likened to a labyrinth in which one despairs of ever finding the exit. Or else it, too, is like a great machine whose ceaseless and inexorable working is beyond human logic and comprehension. The only certainty is fear, the fear instilled by waiting for the impending and inevitable tragedy. It is the fear of the locusts, which everyone knows will come, but when? And what form will the locusts take? Will they be animals or bombs or rays from outer space? The question is not answered by the deadly white ash that flutters down at the close of the play. Although the world may endure (the survival of a little boy would so suggest), the creation of a better planet free of war is not likely: the child is shooting his toy rifle.

Like *Tempo di cavallette, La foresta* was also written in 1956 although it did not reach the stage until three years later, when it was given in German translation at the Staatstheater in Kassel. This seems to have been its only theatrical realization, although Martin Esslin regards it as d'Errico's most important work.[41] Certainly it is the playwright's most original piece, as well as his most universal work. Here, no references to a specific geographic location are made, and those characters who have names have decidedly un-Italian ones—Max, Margot, and Jack (Cric in the original). The forest could be anywhere or nowhere; in fact, its location is metaphysical, because, notwithstanding the presence of moles and mosquitoes, many of its natural features have been metamorphosed by a technological imagination. Mushrooms are steel bolts, tin cans have replaced seashells, and the forest itself consists not of trees but of steel girders and beams. Into this strange world come Max and Margot, fleeing from a nightmarish past much as Pirandello's six characters arrived on stage seeking to concretize their nonexistence as literary characters.

Although the forest lies ostensibly beyond the "real" world and appears at first to offer a kind of refuge to those numbed by the atrocities—most of them caused by war—that lie "outside," in

effect it is a microcosm, a grotesque image of a mechanical civilization and all its dehumanizing aspects carried to the extreme. Its
inhabitants have already been contaminated; they are able to
ignore with consummate indifference the most fundamental
human qualities, they are easily distracted by the radio, by simple
and absurd machines, by their own personal visions of a more
perfect world that is not nor can be. They, no more than those
who dwell outside the forest, cannot solve basic human problems
such as death or the forging of genuine bonds of affection and
understanding. Each—except perhaps for Margot—is isolated in a
personal world. They do form superficial relations among themselves, but ultimately even these seem inhuman. They are much
closer to the necessary relation that exists between the mole and
the mosquito in the forest: the latter feeds on the blood of the
mole, and the mole eats the mosquito in a cyclical and absurd
symbiosis. Such are the inhabitants of the forest; they are the
detritus of a mechanical and dehumanizing world that horrifies
d'Errico. As Esslin writes, *La foresta* "is the passionate outcry of a
romantic against the deadening of sensibilities, the loss of contact
with organic nature, that the spread of a civilization of concrete
and iron has brought about" (213).

Written in 1957, *Il formicaio* is d'Errico's most derivative play.[42]
We mentioned earlier the similarity of its ending with that of
Ionesco's *Les chaises,* but even more sustained comparisons can be
made with Elio Vittorini's fine novel, *Conversazione in Sicilia,*
which, after serialization in 1938–39, was published in book form
in 1941.[43] Revolution is a principal theme in both works, and in
each a vagabond underground revolutionary performs the trade
of and is known as the "Knifegrinder." Moreover, the closing
scene of the play mirrors that of Vittorini's work: in both the
protagonist succeeds in communicating—but not by means of
intelligible verbal language—with everyone present except the
representatives of the police (i.e., the Investigator in d'Errico's
play and the two Fascist undercover policemen in the novel).

The first act opens in Piazza della Libertà and its Caffè Indipen-
denza, a historic café that has been the scene of armed conflict in
1870, 1915, and 1942. At the moment, all the patrons of the café
are lying prone as bullets whine among the overturned tables and
spilled drinks; a madman has barricaded himself in a nearby
garret and is shooting randomly among the crowd. As the au-
thorities close in on him he leaps to his death, and calm returns to
the café and to its half-dozen customers. As in most of d'Errico's
works, some characters have Christian names (Clotilde, Mr. and

Mrs. Romei), others merely descriptive ones—the Investigator, the Neapolitan, the Waiter. These are soon joined by Casimiro, the protagonist of the play; Casimiro is an itinerant street performer who earns his living by playing an ocarina, doing sleight-of-hand tricks, and imitating animal noises as well as performing feats of hypnotism, mind reading, and ventriloquy. He is glib-tongued, mobile, and dressed in a zany fashion. Like Jean Anouilh's hero in *Le voyageur sans bagage* (1936),[44] Casimiro lost his memory during the war; he was found without identification in the bombed-out rubble of a railroad station. "A traveler from nowhere and with nowhere to go" (161), Casimiro leads a free and unfettered life, amusing himself by regarding the rest of civilization as an ant heap: "The city, the ant heap, a nightmare transformed into concrete, steel, glass . . . with the ants running about night and day looking for a crumb of happiness" (159).

Soon after speaking briefly with the subversive Knifegrinder, Casimiro is interrogated by the Investigator who wants to know whether they spoke about knives or other weapons. Led from one cleverly laid trap to another, Casimiro soon realizes that whether their conversation was subversive or innocent is irrelevant. In fact, the Investigator thinks that *not* talking about weapons can be significant. Casimiro is outraged. "Is it a crime to talk with a Knifegrinder without discussing blades and knives? Why, it's monstrous!" To which the Investigator replies in typical d'Errican fashion: "Justice is always monstrous, if only because it is equal for everyone. While each man has his own shoe size, his own wife, and his own favorite drink, . . . when he must give account to the law for his actions, he is confronted by laws that are the same for everyone and, therefore, appropriate for no one" (167). When Casimiro refuses to say anything more, the Investigator threatens him with arrest; the young man, frightened, dashes into the street, where he is struck by a Buick driven by Annalisa, the daughter of the local industrial czar.

Casimiro regains consciousness in a hospital room, the setting for the second scene. Although he was officially dead for eighteen minutes, a surgeon revived him with open heart massage. Unfortunately, Casimiro's guardian angel, believing him to be dead, escaped from his body through the incision and then realized her mistake only after the surgeon had sutured the wound, effectively preventing her reentry into her ward's body. Now she must remain outside, though visible only to Casimiro. The Angel is not a very imposing figure; she is represented as a shy young girl dressed in a rather shabby white gown, down-at-the-heels red slippers, and with dusty, moth-eaten wings. It is she who reveals to Casimiro that his earlier identity was that of the accountant, Lo Guzzo Pettinato.

In this scene we also meet Giorgio, a paralyzed composer confined to a wheelchair and slowly dying of a fatal disease. Giorgio writes popular songs, although his dream is to write a "Hymn of the Barricades," which will be played on the day of revolution. With Casimiro and the Knifegrinder, Giorgio forms the revolutionary triumvirate of the play, though their radicalism, like that of all of d'Errico's revolutionaries, is mild, nonviolent, and more abstract than physical.

The second act finds us once more at the café, in the midst of a fireworks display celebrating the anniversary of some unspecified event: no one knows which one. Casimiro remarks that in their nation (obviously Italy) "every day is the anniversary of some memorable event. Scientific discoveries, won or lost battles, conquered or relinquished empires." And the Neapolitan elaborates: "Making every day a holiday is our way of protesting while still respecting the law. To the questions of earthquakes, wars, and plagues, we answer with fireworks, music in the village squares, and the tarantella" (187). An ensuing conversation between the Investigator and Casimiro turns on the question of the existence of the angel. When a skeptical Investigator dares the Angel to give some concrete proof of her existence, she plants a solid kick to his rear. Outraged, the Investigator hauls everyone off to the police station except Casimiro, who has been standing squarely in front of the Investigator and therefore is above suspicion.

A moment later Giorgio rolls his wheelchair in and as Casimiro goes toward him, he finds his way blocked by a man in a uniform—it is the Knifegrinder, who has renounced his freedom and revolutionary ways in order to conform; he has become a security guard in the abrasives division of the local factory. Casimiro is dumbfounded:

> Casimiro. What happened? [To the Knifegrinder.] Did the Investigator get to you?
> Knifegrinder. [With a sigh.] Maybe . . . But I didn't give up out of fear . . . [He makes a vague gesture.] Fatigue maybe . . . and disappointment.
> Casimiro. [Looking alternately at his two friends.] I don't understand . . . I have been waiting for you to come back . . . And now I hear you talking about disappointment.

Giorgio. It's the ant heap . . . [*He indicates the Knifegrinder.*] He says that the ants don't want either liberty or independence.
Knifegrinder. That's right . . . Half of them long for yesterday's chains, the other half are hoping for the chains of tomorrow. (189–90)

At that point Casimiro notices that the name of the café has been changed: it is now the Caffè Dipendenza. His world is rapidly changing, and it effectively comes to an end after he chides his unconventional Angel for shoplifting, sneaking rides on a merry-go-round, and going to movies without paying:

Casimiro. The world is really in a fix if this is what they teach you in Heaven!
Angel. [*Mortified.*] No . . . I learned these things on Earth . . . But now my vacation is over.
Casimiro. What does that mean?
Angel. I have to leave. An angel cannot stay in this world. (197)

As the ragtag Angel leaves, Annalisa, representative of the established social order, appears. The scene closes with her and Casimiro gazing into each other's eyes, clearly in love.

The final segment of *Il formicaio* opens with the patrons of the café listening to an automobile race on the radio. Then comes the news of Giorgio's death, and soon after Casimiro—or more accurately the accountant Lo Guzzo Pettinato—enters, dressed in a gray suit and bowler hat, the very picture of conformity. His face is waxen, his movements wooden, and his gestures mechanical. Helped onto a table in the café, he begins his speech consisting of repeated nonsense syllables: "To-to . . . Toro-totò." Strangely, the speech has meaning for all except the Investigator. He cannot understand because, as one character explains, the Investigator is an instrument for vindication and nothing else. "The vindication of abstract morality against the concrete individual . . . The defense of a stagnant government against the evolution of those governed" (208). What is Casimiro's message? His listeners give it various interpretations:

Knifegrinder. Everyone is concerned about making objects, no one is worried about not destroying mankind. . . .
Clotilde. He's right! All we do is gulp down our days without chewing them, in a mad dash toward death. . . .
Professor. Revolution is the opiate of the people, because it makes us forget about current problems in order to annul them in a dream of

tomorrow, which never comes true . . . Revolution is a clever smoke-
screen invented by those in power. (207–8)

In short, Casimiro's message as it is interpreted by these listeners
is the same as those that run throughout d'Errico's plays: horror at
the materialism and conformity of modern life, a preference for
gentle, nonviolent anarchy instead of traditional political revolution, and, in the persons of Casimiro and the Knifegrinder, the
difficulty (even impossibility) of maintaining one's individualism.

Despite certain qualities—humor, some effective dramatic devices, and a couple of well-drawn characters such as the Neapolitan and the enchanting figure of the guardian angel—*Il formicaio*
is d'Errico's least satisfying full-length play. It is a play that sets out
to explore two important themes: the identity of the individual
and one's conformity to society. Its treatment of both is superficial
and unconvincing. Casimiro's amnesia is a dubious stratagem that
ultimately has little to do with the play, and the rapid conversions
of Casimiro and especially of the Knifegrinder from anarchists to
extreme conformists strain the credulity of even the experienced
viewer of plays of the absurd. Most disappointingly, the central
metaphor of the work, the metaphor of the ant heap, is never
integrated into the play. Unlike the forest in d'Errico's previous
play, the ant heap remains at all times a literary conceit that never
achieves visual or dramatic realization.

D'Errico's last full-length absurdist drama, conversely, is one of
his finest. Less poetic than *La foresta*—but also less rhetorical and
didactic—*L'assedio* is a carefully composed drama whose characters are integrated into the play in a convincing tangle of human
fears and passions. Its setting, like that of *La foresta*, is a metaphysical dimension, isolated from what is usually called reality,
and yet it is instantly recognizable as a metaphorical locus of
humanity; it is the warehouse of human dreams and desires
concretized in the old and dusty trappings of a ragpicker's place
of business.

It also functions as a summation of d'Errico's themes. The
loneliness of the outsider Chanusky recalls the similar isolation of
Margot and Casimiro. Here too are the ubiquitous individual
obsessions of d'Errico's characters, their human need for the
recognition and acceptance represented by a title or a uniform
that, in a world where individuality has disappeared, becomes a
symbol not only of one's worth but of one's very existence. Such
symbols become a means—however illusory—of defense against
the gear mesh of society that threatens to grind them to

nothingness. Beset by Kafkian fears without name, they can hope in only the future, which always deceives them. It is significant that Isaac first mistakes the Mephistophelian Brandolisio for the Messiah; good in d'Errico's works is found only in the optimistic imagination of certain characters. This imagined good, when and if it finally comes, wears the bitter face of its opposite. Although evil and death are always present in d'Errico's work, good and a life of meaning are forever absent, existing sometimes in the past but more often in a future that inevitably recedes with the passage of time. D'Errico's characters are so many Tantaluses whose imaginations can conceive of happiness but whose grasp always falls short. The universe they inhabit is cruelly ironic, a world that is, when judged by human reason and suffering, irrational and unknowable. It is as horrifying and as incomprehensible as the fact of the siege itself.

What is this universe of d'Errico? How can one describe it? In the plays of d'Errico, the absurdity of the world is most commonly manifest in the presence of a nameless and irrational fear. The characters of *Tempo di cavallette* fear an invasion of locusts, though they are not even sure that locusts exist. The fear is often manifested by a feeling of being cold inside; yet they can explain neither their chills nor fears. As often as not, their fears are unfounded: they have created them to fill the emptiness within themselves. Venturella says in *Qualcuno al cancello:* "The silence. . . . The emptiness. An emptiness that you have to fill in some way, and so you create phantasms and take up the vice of fear" (342). Fear is the dominant mark of d'Errico's characters and of the times in which they live. "The true face of our epoch," says the Hunter in *Tempo di cavallette*, "is fear" (52). To balance this fear, to try, if not to overcome it, at least to neutralize it, all the characters have initially a certain amount of hope. Their hope may be unwarranted, but it is nonetheless tenacious for it stems from those ancient human traits, pride and egoism—the belief of each that the others may well be doomed but that somehow things will be different for *him.*

Thus, each goes on hoping. And for what? For deliverance. They hope to stumble on something that will give them freedom or identity, or they expect someone outside themselves to save them from their human condition. Each waits for his personal Godot. In *L'assedio,* Isaac watches for the coming of God, and Chanusky is waiting for a prize of some kind, of any kind; still others spend their time searching among the rags in a warehouse, hoping to find a sailor's suit or the red jacket of a jazz musician. In

La foresta the poet dreams of an impossible utopia, and Max expects to find a way out of the forest. The Professor hears voices; others are content with an old tin can that, when held to the ear like a seashell, seems to emit a sound. The Professor finally understands that hope of salvation is an illusion:

> We realize that a seashell or a tin can gives off the same humming sound. . . . The humming of our own ears. . . . And the same thing happens with the other voices. Who called me? No one . . . It would be too beautiful, it would be a miracle. We all wait for it, but they are only internal voices, the gurglings of our imagination, acoustic illusions, hope that something will finally reach us from outside. But nothing ever happens. From our birth to our death, nothing! (92)

No salvation from absurdity is possible. One can escape from the forest only on the train that stops there once in a while—but the conductor of the train is Death. D'Errico's characters are helpless; life, says the Professor, is against everyone. It is a spider web, "and the more you struggle to escape, the more entangled you become. . . . A spider web . . . and all of us are caught in it" (93–94). Consciously or unconsciously, d'Errico's characters eventually become insensible to their condition. Indeed, they can endure only if they become numb, indifferent toward God, nature, their fellow human beings, and finally even themselves.

D'Errico does not limit himself to a description of the absurd condition of human existence. If life and the world were once beautiful—and this is a recurring theme in d'Errico's plays—what has gone wrong? What are the origins of the apparently inevitable alienation that his characters experience? D'Errico perceives in men and women a fundamental disharmony that becomes more pronounced as they evolve. The disharmony is evident in the incongruity between their biologic needs and their spiritual qualities. As Max in *La foresta* says: "Even poets have to eat every day. This, you see, is one of the many imperfections of Creation. A handsome young man is born with the heart of a poet, but with a stomach that has to be filled three times a day" (107). In the same play, at the moment of his death, the Professor experiences the total absurdity of the human condition: "Do you think I asked to be put together in this stupid way, with the same needs as beasts but with a brain that can conceive of the fourth dimension?" (112). Human beings are a mistake; the very term "human" is synonymous with imperfection. To think of people as machines, as

d'Errico often does, one might say that alienation has been pro-
grammed into them. "There must be," maintains the Clerk in
Tempo di cavallette, "a flaw somewhere in the way things are put
together, or else there is a curse inside us, an original sin that
cannot be washed away" (19). In *L'assedio* the old man Isaac re-
minds Chanusky not to forget that he is only matter. Chanusky
proudly replies that this point is true, but he is living *human*
matter. Isaac agrees: "Right. And therefore you are an incomplete
creature. A disharmony, a mistake. If I weren't afraid of offending you, I would call you a monstrosity" (223). The old man
elaborates on the origins of the human species: "Go back to the
beginning and you will find God. It is with him that you have to
settle up. . . . The one who made the first puppet—out of mud,
naturally. He looked at it from all angles, then he said: 'Well, it
didn't turn out as I had hoped. But it's too late now.' He breathed
life into its nostrils and then off he went about his other business"
(224). People are damned from creation and there is no hope of
perfectibility. Chanusky asks: "Don't you think that the puppet, in
time, might improve?" Isaac replies: "For thousands of years the
waves have beat upon the reefs, and they fall back shattered into
spray that the sand reabsorbs. Each new crest thinks it is the
strongest, the breaker that will smash everything. Illusions! . . .
Maybe men just haven't understood things yet. . . . Maybe at the
root of everything there is a mistake, a misunderstanding" (224).
The original mistake of which Isaac speaks recalls the Christian
doctrine of original sin. The difference, however, is that the
former is not a sin attributable to human will but a fact of existence. Although several of d'Errico's characters argue from a
Christian viewpoint, the question of the existence of God is ultimately insignificant; whether one explains the malediction in
Christian terms or in the terms of Darwinian evolution, the fact
remains unchanged.

In *La foresta* the General approaches the question of human
origins from the viewpoint of evolution. The General's passion is
building machines that perform no work: they move, they are
fascinating to watch, but they have no practical application. Their
raison d'être is that they give "a sense of well-being, of confidence,
as does everything that is the result of a mathematical calculation. . . . They console man for his imperfection" (134). Indeed,
the General defines humans as creatures who make machines.
When Jack, a service station attendant, objects that there must

have been a time when people lived without machines, the General traces the origin of the wheel.

> *General.* Yes, after the chaos . . . When men and beasts were one and the same, and they ate each other by turns, and they slept in caves or in trees. But one day, a living being very much like all the other monkeys managed, with some sharp rocks, to slice the trunk of a tree . . . The wheel was born, and with that the monkey had become a man.
> *Jack.* The Vinedresser says God was the one who made men different from the beasts.
> *General.* Could be, but the first sign of that difference was without a doubt the wheel. And from that day on, man has not been able to do without machines . . . he has kept on making increasingly perfect ones. (134)

Two possible explanations, then, for the origin of the human condition of absurdity are that either God erred in his creation, or else a flaw occurred in the evolutionary process. In either case, human beings are imperfect creatures who are driven to seek perfection in the machines that they build.

Similarly, d'Errico foresees two possible conclusions to human life and the absurd world that sustains it. Neither is reassuring, for both end in destruction. In *L'assedio* the Reporter declares that the increasing insensibility of human beings is nature's way of preparing them for the end of the world. The Old Man in *La panchina* also foresees the end of the world, and he offers an apocalyptic vision reminiscent of the final pages of Italo Svevo's *La coscienza di Zeno:* people themselves, apparently through their technology, will destroy the earth.[45] The alternative consequence of alienation is perhaps even more horrifying. In *La foresta* d'Errico advances the idea that machines will someday assume our human qualities. The General states that all machines—even useless ones like his own—are working against us: "That's precisely why useless machines are so useful . . . They fascinate whoever looks at them, they give a rhythm to thoughts and slowly neutralize them" (122). Max foresees that, after having taken over the faculty of thinking, machines will eventually suffer for us: "Cybernetics . . . the last hope of mankind. After they have done our thinking for us, someday machines will do our suffering for us" (123). And the General and Max envision a future in which human beings will be supplanted by mechanical ones:

General. [*Smiling.*] All of us are little cogwheels, and we can't get out of the gearworks.

Max. The future generations will be nothing but gearworks; they'll go around arm in arm with robots.

General. Then the robots will get the upper hand, stage a coup d'état, and subjugate mankind. The world will be ruled by robots.

Max. They'll take the place of God; they will recreate and organize a cosmos according to the laws of mathematical calculation. Maybe that is the goal and raison d'être of tomorrow's generations. (136–37)

Although d'Errico proposed alternative explanations for the origins and the consequences of absurdity, two points emerge clearly. First, the origins of human beings are such that their alienation is inevitable; second, the consequences of this alienation will eventually render them completely insensible. Supposing that the world does not perish in a final cataclysm, what will be the condition of the human race when it is subservient to machines? When any rapport between people and the world that surrounds them no longer exists, when the last hope is gone and they can no longer even suffer, they will be left only with their biologic senses and needs. They may not be sleeping in caves, but, having lost their sense of self, having become indifferent toward their origins, their condition, and their destiny, humans will be once more indistinguishable from the beasts. Evolution will have completed another cycle, a new selection of species will have occurred, and people, as we know them today, will be extinct. Ezio d'Errico's theater of the absurd reflects the pale twilight of the human species. It is a theater to which the Professor's dying words in *La foresta* could aptly serve as an epigraph: "I see night falling, and I know there will be no dawn" (113).

Like most examples of the theater of the absurd, d'Errico's theater is unrelentingly cynical. Indeed, pessimism, or at the very least a bitter cynicism, informed most of his works and even his life. Yet neither his view of the world as a cruel and absurd contradiction nor his failure to achieve sufficient recognition for his achievements could destroy what Calendoli has called his "profound sense of humanity."[46] In the works of d'Errico an intense love of life is present and indomitable even when faced with the absurdity of the human condition. D'Errico resists; without rage or bitterness, he carried on his revolt in a determined and assured way, like the stoic that he was. Indeed, his self-composed epitaph reads: "Stoically as he lived so did he pass away." In similar fashion he patiently endured the lack of recognition accorded to his works. "A great calm has descended upon me," he told an interviewer in 1961. "Among other benefits, my new theater has reinforced my conviction that the important thing is to create something that will last. The performance [of my plays] interests me only slightly. The work, unlike the author, can wait. And it is the work that counts."[47]

The plays that follow will give ample evidence that the work of Ezio d'Errico has waited long enough. It is time now to recognize d'Errico's contribution to twentieth-century theater and to assign to the Italian playwright his due position among the dramatists of the theater of the absurd.

Notes

1. Ossia Trilling, "Ezio d'Errico—A New Pirandello?" *Theatre World* 54 (April 1958): 41.

2. *Qualcuno al cancello* (Someone at the gate) was staged at Sarezzo in March 1971. For places and dates of other performances, see the bibliography.

3. Francesco Callari, "Rappresentato a Vienna con Genet e Ionesco: D'Errico non è profeta in patria," *Corriere Lombardo* (Milan) 4–5 April 1961. Similar laments about Italy's neglect of d'Errico can be found in Federico Doglio, "D'Errico o del virtuosismo," *Studi Cattolici* 5 (November–December 1961): 51, 55. Reprint, *Il Dramma* 38 (February 1962): 45–46. See also Italo Alighiero Chiusano, "Riascoltiamo le molte voci di Ezio d'Errico," *Il Dramma* 48 (June 1972): 13. All translations are my own.

4. Aldo Capasso, "Un dramma di Ezio d'Errico," *Realismo Lirico*, n.s. 40 (July–August 1960): 36.

5. Juan Guerrero Zamora, *Historia del teatro contemporaneo*, 4 vols. (Barcelona: Juan Flors, 1961–67), 2:95–97.

6. Martin Esslin, *The Theatre of the Absurd*, Rev. ed. (Woodstock, N.Y.: Overlook Press, 1973), 211–13.

7. Georges Sonnier, "Un teatro della solitudine," *Il Dramma* 37 (August–September 1961): 63–64. Also in *Tempo di cavallette, La foresta, Il formicaio* (Bologna: Cappelli, 1962), 5.

8. D'Errico, *Parabole 1937* (Milan: Sperling & Kupfer, 1937).

9. D'Errico, *Da liberati* (Modena: Guanda, 1939).

10. Giovanni Calendoli, "L'opera può attendere perché l'opera resta," *L'Italia Che Scrive* 15 (April 1972): 31.

11. General Antonio d'Errico (brother of Ezio), personal interview, 27 June 1987.

12. D'Errico, *Noi due disarmati* (Rome: O. E. T., Edizioni del Secolo, 1946).

13. See Vinicio Marinucci, "Un uomo-record che scrive, dipinge, combatte," *Momento Sera* (Rome), 26 February 1959; "Ezio d'Errico," *Studi Cattolici* 5 (November–December 1961): 53; and Giovanni Calendoli, "Esperienze e traguardi di d'Errico drammaturgo," *L'Italia Che Scrive* 15 (April 1972): 31.

14. Vice [pseud.], *L'Unità* (Milan), 19 December 1953; Guido Albani, "Set-

timana di novità," *Oggi* (31 December 1953): 41–42; Eligio Posssenti, *Corriere della Sera* (Milan), 19 December 1953; Aldo Capasso, "La 'Sei giorni' di Ezio d'Errico," *Realismo Lirico* (6 January 1954): 51–56.

15. Leonida Rèpaci, "*L'oggetto* di Ezio d'Errico," *Teatro d'ogni tempo* (Milan: Ceschina, 1967), 818.

16. D'Errico, "Lettera aperta," *Maschere*, n.s. (April 1962): 43–44.

17. Esslin, *Theatre of the Absurd*, 5.

18. Ibid., 7.

19. Ibid., 213.

20. Eugène Ionesco, *Les chaises*, in *Théâtre*, 5 vols. (Paris: Gallimard, 1954–74), 1:172.

21. D'Errico, *Il formicaio*, in *Teatro dell'assurdo* (Turin: Edizioni dell'Albero, 1968) 206–12. Subsequent citations from this work are noted parenthetically in the text.

22. Henri Bergson, *Le rire: Essai sur la signification du comique*, 82d ed. (Paris: Presses Universitaires de France, 1947), 29.

23. Alberto Perrini, "Ionesco a Napoli, d'Errico a Darmstadt," *Lo Specchio* (Rome), 8 December 1960.

24. Giorgio Prosperi, "Un epigono del primo '900," *Ridotto* 22 (May 1972): 4–5.

25. C. F., "Il 'teatro dell'assurdo' di Ezio d'Errico," *Ridotto* 14 (March 1964): 48.

26. See n. 7.

27. Mario Apollonio, "Cronache e testi della drammaturgia corale," *Humanitas* 6 (June 1964): 670.

28. Aldo Capasso, "Volti e volto di Ezio d'Errico," *Teatro Scenario* 16 (1952): 14.

29. D'Errico, "Il messaggio dell'imperatore," *Il Dramma* 39 (April 1963): 38.

30. Ibid.

31. Umberto Eco, *Opera aperta: Forma e indeterminazione nelle poetiche contemporanee* (Milan: Bompiani, 1962).

32. D'Errico, "Opere aperte e chiuse," *Il Dramma* 38 (August–September 1962): 72.

33. Ibid., 74.

34. D'Errico, "Messaggio," 38.

35. D'Errico, "Risposta all'inchiesta sullo stato basso del teatro contemporaneo," in *Il Dramma* 37 (November 1961): 54.

36. Quoted in C. F., "Il 'teatro dell'assurdo'," 47.

37. D'Errico, "Messaggio," 40.

38. D'Errico, "Il teatro dell'assurdo," *Il Dramma* 38 (June 1962): 40.

39. Italo Alighiero Chiusano, "Germania: Una novità assoluta di Ezio d'Errico al teatro di Kassel," *Il Dramma* 35 (October 1959): 43.

40. Trilling, "A New Pirandello," 41.

41. Esslin, *Theatre of the Absurd*, 212.

42. According to information in the Cappelli edition of *Tempo di cavallette, La foresta, il formicaio*, the play was translated into French, German, Spanish, and English. I have been unable, however, to find its English version. To my knowledge, the play was never performed.

43. First published as *Nome e lagrime* in Florence by Parenti; later editions by Bompiani (Milan, 1942, 1953) carried the title *Conversazione in Sicilia*. Translated into English as *In Sicily* by Wilfred David, with an introduction by Ernest Hemingway (New York: New Directions, 1949).

44. Jean Anouilh, *Le voyageur sans bagage*, in *Pièces noires* (Paris: Calmann-

Lévy, 1945). Translated into English as *Traveller Without Luggage* by John Whiting (London: Methuen, 1959).

45. Italo Svevo, *La coscienza di Zeno* (Bologna: Cappelli, 1923). *Confessions of Zeno,* trans. Beryl de Zoete (New York: Vintage, 1958).

46. Calendoli, "Esperienze e traguardi," 31.

47. "Sette domande all'autore," *Studi Cattolici* 5 (November–December 1961): 54.

Select Bibliography

Primary Sources

Ezio d'Errico wrote numerous novels, stories, and scripts for films, radio, and television; none of these is included in the list that follows. This bibliography contains only certain selected essays on the theater and the plays that he wrote for the stage. The order of information for the latter is: Italian title; English equivalent (italicized if the translation has been published); date of composition (if significantly different from the first date of presentation, publication, or prize award); director, theater, city, and date of first performance if known; publication data; and drama prizes won by the work. All are full-length plays unless otherwise indicated.

PLAYS

Un uomo in più (One man too many). Dir. Giovanni Orsini. Teatro Sant'Erasmo, Milan. 26 November 1948. Scuola del Teatro Drammatico Prize, 1948.

L'oggetto (The object). Dir. Luigi Squarzina. Teatro Ateneo, Rome. 12 April 1949. *Teatro* 2 (25 May 1950): 19–33. Second prize, Concorso Riccione, 1949.

L'uomo della luce (The man from the light company). Dir. Giulio Donadio. Teatro Olimpia, Milan. 11 September 1950. *Teatro* 2 (20 October 1950): 17–32.

Ricordo dell'avvenire (Memory of the future). Dir. Ezio d'Errico. Teatro delle Arti, Rome. 9 November 1950. English trans. in *Italian Theatre Review/Revue du Théâtre Italien* 2 (May–August 1953).

Buio dentro (The dark inside). Dir. Gaspare Gozzi. Teatro dei Satiri, Rome. 24 January 1951. *Teatro Scenario* 15 (1 March 1951): 19–30.

La dama di cuori (The queen of hearts). Dir. Ernesto Sabbatini. Teatro Quirino, Rome. 9 April 1951. *Teatro Scenario* 15 (1 November 1951): 17–32.

Cordone sanitario (Sanitary cordon). Dir. Ezio d'Errico. Teatro Civico, La Spezia. 16 July 1951.

Barbablù (Bluebeard). Dir. Michele Abruzzo. Teatro Comunale, Cesena. 1 January 1952.

La corona di carta (The paper crown). Dir. Vincenzo Tieri. Teatro Mercadante, Naples. 5 April 1952. *Teatro Scenario* 16 (1 July 1952): 17–30.

Incontro coi superstiti (Encounter with the survivors). Pesaro, 5 June 1958. *Ridotto* 8 (June 1958): 19–39. Premio Pirandello, 1953.

Quelli di sotto (The people downstairs). Dir. Livio and Guido Merico. Teatro Astral, Buenos Aires. 8 June 1953.

John. Dir. Carlo Di Stefano. Teatro Novelli, Rimini. 17 July 1953. *Ridotto* 4 (1 January 1954).

Salita all'inferno (Ascent into hell). Dir. Claudio Fino. Teatro Olimpia, Milan. 22 September 1953. *Teatro Scenario* 17 (1 December 1953): 17–30.

La sei giorni (The six-day race). Dir. Giorgio Strehler. Piccolo Teatro, Milan. 18 December 1953. *Teatro Scenario* 18 (1 April 1954): 45–62. English trans. in *Italian Theatre Review/Revue du Théâtre Italien* 2 (November–December 1953): 23–49. Concorso Istituto del Dramma Italiano-Piccolo Teatro Prize.

Quelli dell'armadio a specchio (The ones in the wardrobe). Dir. Giuseppe Di Martino. Teatro Ridotto, Venice. 15 January 1955.

L'amante in città (The lover in the city). Dir. Carlo Lodovici. Teatro Nuovo, Trieste. 1 February 1955. *Teatro Scenario* 19 (1 December 1955): 47–61.

Best Seller. Dir. Ezio d'Errico. Piccolo Teatro, Turin. 2 February 1956. *Il Dramma* 32 (March 1956): 9–28.

Tempo di cavallette (The year of the locusts). Written 1956. Dir. Werner Düggelin. Landestheater, Darmstadt, Germany. 6 March 1958. *Il Dramma* 34 (June 1958): 8–38.

Viaggio di nozze (Honeymoon). Dir. Daniele D'Anza. Teatro delle Arti, Rome. 20 April 1956. *Ridotto* 7 (September 1957): 19–40.

La foresta (The forest). Written 1956. Dir. Albert Fischel. Staatstheater, Kassel, Germany. 19 September 1959. *Il Dramma* 35 (November 1959): 8–33.

Le forze (The powers). Written 1957. Dir. Fantasio Piccoli. Piccolo Teatro, Bolzano. 22 March 1965. *Il Dramma* 33 (June 1957): 5–27. Premio Napoli, 1957.

Il formicaio (The ant heap). Written 1957.

Incontro col gentleman (Encounter with a gentleman). One act. Dir. Renato Lelli. Teatro Minimo, Bologna. 5 May 1959. *Il Dramma* 35 (June 1959): 61–65.

Segreto di famiglia (Family secret). One act. Dir. Enrico Romero. Teatro Pirandello, Rome. 11 September 1958.

L'assedio (The siege). Written 1959. Dir. Benozzo Conti. Teatro San

Silvestro, Livorno. 4 January 1973. *Il Dramma* 36 (November 1960): 5–36. Premio Riccione, 1960.

Qualcuno al cancello (Someone at the gate). Written 1960. Sarezzo. 27 March 1971. *Il Dramma* 37 (August–September 1961): 65–90.

La panchina (The parkbench). One act. Written 1961. Piccolo Teatro, Arezzo. 19 April 1964. *Il Dramma* 38 (December 1962): 78–86.

Il viaggio (The trip). One act. Dir. Claudio Frosi. Teatro dell'Orologio, Rome. 1988. *Maschere*, n.s. (April 1962): 51–62.

Dove siamo (The point where we are). One act. *Il Dramma* 38 (May 1962): 21–32.

La sedia a dondolo (The rocking chair). One act. Dir. Claudio Frosi. Teatro dell'Orologio, Rome. 1988. *Il Dramma* 39 (March 1963): 54–60.

La visita (The examination). One act. *Maschere*, n.s. (May–June 1963): 37–48.

L'operazione (The operation). One act. Teatro de' Servi, Rome. 3 November 1971. *Il Dramma* 40 (February 1964): 39–45.

Romanzo d'appendice (Serial novel). One act. *Ridotto* 14 (April 1964): 37–42.

Conversazione con Wladimiro (Conversation with Vladimir). One act. Hunter College Theater, New York. 23 May 1971. *Il Dramma* 40 (May 1964): 27–31.

Balthazar. Written before 1962. *Il Dramma* 41 (February 1965): 15–41.

L'incidente (The accident). One act. *Il Dramma* 43 (February–March 1967): 88–94.

COLLECTED PLAYS

Tempo di cavallette, La foresta, Il formicaio. Introduction by Georges Sonnier. Bologna: Cappelli, 1962.

Teatro dell'assurdo. Introduction by Italo Alighiero Chiusano. Turin: Edizioni dell'Albero, 1968. Contains: *Tempo di cavallette, La foresta, Il formicaio, L'assedio, La panchina, Dove siamo, La sedia a dondolo, Conversazione con Wladimiro*, bibliography.

ESSAYS

"Risposta all'inchiesta 'Il teatro e lo stato: Controllo o libertà.'" *Il Dramma* 27 (1 November 1951): 59.

"I miei amici critici." *Teatro Scenario* 16 (1 March 1952): 44–47.
"Lo spettatore d'oggi." *Teatro Scenario* 16 (15 June 1952): 7.
"I 'partigiani' del teatro." *Ridotto* 6 (December 1956): 8–9.
"Registrazione su nastro." *Ridotto* 7 (July–August 1957): 7–8.
"Filodrammatica in pista." *Ridotto* 7 (December 1957): 6–7.
"La nostra triste corrida." *Il Dramma* 37 (March 1961): 66–67.
"Risposta all'inchiesta sullo stato basso del teatro contemporaneo."
   Il Dramma 37 (November 1961): 53–54.
"La via difficile." *Il Dramma* 37 (December 1961): 45–47.
"Lettera aperta." *Maschere,* n.s. (April 1962): 43–50.
"Il teatro dell'assurdo." *Il Dramma* 38 (June 1962): 38–40.
"Opere aperte e chiuse." *Il Dramma* 38 (August–Sept. 1962): 72–
   76.
"Utilità dei concorsi: Esperienze di un giudice." *Il Dramma* 38
   (October 1962): 62–65.
"Il messaggio dell'imperatore." *Il Dramma* 39 (April 1963): 38–43.
"Un secolo fa e oggi." *Ridotto* 14 (April 1964): 3–4.
"Teatro e comunità." *Il Dramma* 40 (September 1964): 40–41.
"Critico e autore." *Ridotto* 15 (January–February 1965): 3–4.
"Non ce l'abbiamo con nessuno." *Ridotto* 20 (January 1970): 2–4.

Secondary Sources

The following select bibliography contains only articles and books that relate to d'Errico's theater of the absurd or to his life, thought, and works in general. Reviews and studies of his early theatrical works and nontheatrical writings have been omitted.

A. M. "Molti gli applausi per *L'assedio.*" *Il Telegrafo* (Livorno), 7
   January 1973.
Andreucci, Costanza. "Ricordo di Ezio d'Errico." *Costume* 3 (July–
   September 1972): 4.
Apollonio, Mario. "Cronache e testi della drammaturgia corale."
   Humanitas 6 (June 1964): 664–78.
Barbiera, Gianfranco. "Ha suscitato qualche perplessità *La pan-
   china* di Ezio d'Errico." *Nazione-Sera* (Florence), 22 April 1964.
Calendoli, Giovanni. "Esperienze e traguardi di d'Errico dram-
   maturgo." *L'Italia Che Scrive* 15 (April 1972): 31.
———. "L'opera può attendere perché l'opera resta." *L'Italia Che
   Scrive* 15 (April 1972): 31.
Càllari, Francesco. "Rappresentato a Vienna con Genet e Ionesco:

D'Errico non è profeta in patria." *Corriere Lombardo* (Milan), 4–5 April 1961.

Camilleri, Andrea. "Ezio d'Errico." In *Enciclopedia dello spettacolo*, 4:506–507. 9 vols. Rome: Le Maschere, 1954–1962.

Capasso, Aldo. "Un dramma di Ezio d'Errico." *Realismo Lirico*, n.s. 40 (July–August 1960): 36–43.

———. "Volti e volto di Ezio d'Errico." *Teatro Scenario* 16 (1952): 13–15.

Cardia, Fiorella. "Ezio d'Errico: Un autore non valorizzato." *Scena Illustrata* 123 (May 1988): 41.

C. F. "Il 'teatro dell'assurdo' di Ezio d'Errico." *Ridotto* 14 (March 1964): 47–48.

Chiusano, Italo Alighiero. "Germania: Una novità assoluta di Ezio d'Errico al teatro di Kassel." *Il Dramma* 35 (October 1959): 43–45.

———. "Invito alla contemplazione." *Il Dramma* 36 (November 1960): 5–9.

———. "Una nuova commedia di Ezio d'Errico al 'Landestheater' di Darmstadt." *Il Dramma* 34 (April 1958): 45–46.

———. "Riascoltiamo le molte voci di Ezio d'Errico." *Il Dramma* 48 (June 1972): 13.

Doglio, Federico. "D'Errico o del virtuosismo." *Studi Cattolici* 5 (November–December 1961): 51, 55. Reprint. *Il Dramma* 38 (February 1962): 45–46.

Esslin, Martin. *The Theatre of the Absurd.* rev. ed. Woodstock, N.Y.: Overlook, 1973.

"Ezio d'Errico." *Italian Theatre Review/Revue du Théâtre Italien* 2 (November–December 1953): 20–21.

"Ezio d'Errico." *Studi Cattolici* 5 (November–December 1961): 53.

Federici, Mario. "Caro Ezio." *Ridotto* 22 (May 1972): 3.

Guerrero Zamora, Juan. *Historia del teatro contemporaneo*, 2: 95–97. 4 vols. Barcelona: Juan Flors, 1961–67.

Heiney, Donald. *America in Modern Italian Literature.* New Brunswick, N.J.: Rutgers University Press, 1964.

Jacobbi, Ruggero. "Quattro scrittori per un teatro impossibile: Ezio d'Errico, Dino Buzzati, Ennio Flaiano, Vincenzo Talarico." In *Teatro Italiano '72: Annuario dell'Istituto del Dramma Italiano*, 151–56. Rome: Bardi, 1973.

Kibler, Louis. "Gentle Anarchy: Ezio d'Errico's Theater of the Absurd." In *Italiana 1987: Selected Papers from the Proceedings of the Fourth Annual Conference of the American Association of Teachers of Italian; November 20–22, 1987; Atlanta, Ga.*, 299–308. Rosary

College Italian Studies 2. River Forest, Ill.: Rosary College, 1989.

Marinucci, Vinicio. "Un uomo-record che scrive, dipinge, combatte." *Momento Sera* (Rome), 26 February 1959.

Monotti, Francesco. "Un personaggio." *Ridotto* 22 (May 1972): 7–8.

Nicolaj, Aldo. "Ricordo di Ezio." *Ridotto* 22 (May 1972): 6.

Perrini, Alberto. "Ionesco a Napoli, d'Errico a Darmstadt." *Lo Specchio* (Rome), 8 December 1960.

Prosperi, Giorgio. "Un epigono del primo '900." *Ridotto* 22 (May 1972): 4–5.

Rèpaci, Leonida. "'L'oggetto' di Ezio d'Errico." In *Teatro d'ogni tempo*, 818–21. Milan: Ceschina, 1967.

"Schede critiche." *Studi Cattolici* 5 (November–December 1961): 52.

Seelmann-Eggebert, Ulrich. "L'attualità e i nuovi autori tedeschi." *Sipario* 13 (April 1958): 18–19.

"Sette domande all'autore." *Studi Cattolici* 5 (November–December 1961): 54.

Sonnier, Georges. "Un teatro della solitudine." *Il Dramma* 37 (August–September 1961): 63–64. Reprint. *Tempo di cavallette, La foresta, Il formicaio*, 5–7. Bologna: Cappelli, 1962.

Torresani, Sergio. "Denuncia e pietá nel teatro di Ezio d'Errico." *Vita e Pensiero* 48 (September 1965): 694–708.

———. "Ezio d'Errico." In *Il teatro italiano negli ultimi vent'anni (1945–1965)*, 175–81. Cremona: Mangiarotti, 1965.

Trilling, Ossia. "Ezio d'Errico—A New Pirandello?" *Theatre World* (London) 54 (April 1958): 41.

Valcini, Alceo. "*Le cavallette* di Ezio d'Errico a Vienna." *Il Dramma* 37 (April 1961): 47.

The Forest

A Dramatic Vision in Two Acts

by
Ezio d'Errico

Edited by Louis Kibler
Translated by John Michael Stuart and Louis Kibler

Characters

Max
Jack
Boy
Margot
Professor
Vinedresser
Conductor
General

ACT 1

SCENE 1

With the curtain still closed, the house lights dim; a musical prelude begins and gradually increases in volume. It is a barbarous symphony of the cries of shackled people, cascading water, and rolls of thunder. Then the music subsides, and the curtain opens. A leafy forest appears projected on a scrim; it is conceived in the exaggerated manner of a seventeenth-century engraving.

The music decreases to a murmur, and the air is pervaded by the sound of birds twittering; this gradually replaces the music until, along with the light, it fades into darkness and silence.

In this darkness the scrim disappears, and in what little visibility is permitted by the obscurity enveloping the stage, one has the impression of a flat countryside with scattered, withered trees.

Dawn breaks, and it gradually becomes easier to distinguish what appear to be trees but are actually architectural elements, metallic constructions, and debris from a mechanical civilization: the tall, slender fragment of a tumbledown house; the trestle of a crane, from whose skeletonlike arm dangle streamers of steel cables; a crumbled smokestack; the frame of an old artesian well; a gallows with the noose still knotted at the end of its crossbeam; some telegraph poles; and downstage an old-fashioned gasoline pump.

All these elements are lined up in perspective on a flat area, the boundaries of which are lost in the darkness, as though the footlights failed to reach the back of the stage; taken as a whole, they form a squalid, surrealistic forest of concrete and metal, in the clearings of which appear bits of stubble, piles of rock, and old, rusty tin cans.

In the foreground, to the right of the audience, is set up a camping tent, out of which comes a middle-aged man (Max) wearing a sand-colored shirt with the sleeves rolled up and Zouave-style pants with puttees.

The man yawns, looks around, discovers a human figure (Jack) squatting down near the gasoline pump, and heads in that direction. Jack is wearing the worn-out overalls of a mechanic and has a cap with a visor.

Max. Good morning.
Jack. [*Staring straight ahead without moving.*] Good morning, sir.
Max. [*Pulling out his pipe and starting to fill it.*] Nice day.

Jack. Not bad. But the wind's from the southeast, and that means rain.

Max. Well then, let's hope the wind changes.

Jack. For this time of year, rain's better. If the wind changes, we're in for a storm.

Max. [*Laughing ironically.*] The "storm of Hell" . . . [*He pauses, then merely for something to say:*] Already on the job at this hour?

Jack. I'm on the job every hour of the day.

Max. And who do you sell gas to?

Jack. Nobody.

Max. That's what I thought. There sure aren't any automobiles around here.

Jack. There used to be. When we still had the road.

Max. Why on earth does your boss insist on keeping a gasoline pump where there aren't any roads?

Jack. He's a very rich man, he owns hundreds of pumps . . . He probably forgot about this one.

Max. And you haven't moved? Haven't you done anything about it?

Jack. [*Shrugging his shoulders.*] The day my boss remembers about me he'll have to give me my back pay. It's written on page fourteen of the work contract.

Max. Let's hope so. [*Pause.*] And you don't get tired of being by yourself all day?

Jack. I was tired from the start. Do you think motorists wanted to waste their time keeping me company? They'd fill up and drive off. [*Pause.*] Anyway, with a little good will, you can always find some way to pass the time.

Max. How?

Jack. [*Pulling out a harmonica from the small pocket of his overalls.*] With this . . . [*He puts the instrument to his lips and plays a few soft, sad sounds on it.*]

Max. Sounds like a cat yowling.

Jack. It's music to me. [*Putting the harmonica back in his pocket.*] But not songs . . . No, it's thoughts, memories . . . colored lights coming out of the throat.

Max. When you're tired of playing music, what do you do?

Jack. I watch the forest grow. I've seen it rise up little by little out of nothing.

Max. Was it fun?

Jack. Fun enough . . . Especially in the spring, when the ground cracks open, and the bolts start cropping up. Then they blossom. In the center of each bolt two little curved pieces of steel sprout forth which grow longer, intertwine . . .

Max. And form grating.

Jack. The embryo of grating. [*Pause.*] The concrete, however, grows like mold, a dirty mold that rises up, separates into layers, and takes over everything. Or else it climbs up crags and outcroppings . . . [*Pause.*] I don't like concrete . . . it makes you think of tombs.

Max. Yeah, but everything around here is only half done. [*Nodding toward the forest.*] Nothing gets finished.

Jack. [*With a slight groan.*] That's exactly how it is. I keep hoping the smokestack will continue on up and start smoking. Or that the well motor will start running . . . Nothing! Everything's always not quite finished.

Max. Anyway, you don't intend to spend your life watching the forest grow, do you?

Jack. What else can I do? Sometimes I make it as far as the river, just to stretch my legs . . . but that makes things even worse. You start to think about a trip that's impossible to make, and you get depressed.

Max. How come?

Jack. When you don't have a boat, hell, not even a rowboat, it's dumb to think of continuing on up the river.

Max. You could build a raft.

Jack. What with? There's nothing here but steel and concrete. [*Pointing.*] There's not much wood in the gallows . . . and who would want to touch it, anyway?

Max. [*Becoming nervous.*] I see. But doesn't the silence get to you? Never talking to anyone . . .

Jack. Oh, but I do.

Max. [*Restless.*] With people who're alive?

Jack. Sure, they're alive. I've got some friends . . . There's the vinedresser, the professor . . . and even a general. [*With sincere admiration.*] A real general, who treats me like a friend. [*Smiling.*] He'll say to me, "Hi, Jack! How's it going?" [*Pause.*] Jack, that's me.

Max. Short for James?

Jack. No. They call me that because of . . . [*He pauses, then makes the motions of raising and lowering a lever.*] The thing you lift automobiles with . . . Ever since I was a boy they called me that. I used to work for a mechanic; I was skinny, and my bones made a cracking sound when I moved.

Max. So that's how you got the nickname!

Jack. Yeah . . . Then I left the mechanic and got a job pumping
gas. At first in the middle of town, then on the outskirts, then
farther and farther away . . . away from my boss. But my boss
kept up with me everywhere . . . he'd spy on me, try to catch me
making a mstake . . . even at night. [*Suddenly upset.*] And I did
everything, you know? I did everything to keep from . . .

Max. [*Coldly.*] I didn't ask you anything.

Jack. [*Humbly.*] I'm sorry. [*He listens. The grumblings of a saxophone
are heard, as if someone were trying out the instrument; then the* Boy
*enters from the left. He is an attractive youth with a boyish face but a
well-developed body. He wears gray velvet pants and a blue sailor's
sweater. The* Boy *slowly crosses the stage, speaking respectfully to an
invisible companion. The words of the invisible speaker are replaced by
notes played softly on an unaccompanied saxophone. This produces a
grotesque and dramatic dialogue that is nonetheless perfectly com-
prehensible. During this action* Jack *remains motionless, staring into
space.* Max, *however, slowly turns to follow the crossing of the two
characters.*]

Boy. [*With polite respect.*] I can assure you, sir, that I'm a hard
worker . . . Don't look at my eyes, which perhaps right now have
the expression of a dog's pupils . . . a starved, greedy dog that
fears and hopes. Don't look at them. I'm a hard worker, and
even though I don't know shorthand . . . [*The saxophone interrupts, muttering two or three notes as if annoyed.*] Oh, but I can learn
it . . . I'll start taking shorthand lessons immediately, no, shorthand *and* typing lessons . . . and if there's an even more complicated way of writing, I'll learn it. [*The saxophone becomes
impatient.*] I see . . . you could easily find employees who're
more experienced, more skilled, who're familiar with complicated bookkeeping and who don't have hangdog eyes; but my
mother told me you were such a powerful and understanding
person. [*The saxophone nervously breaks into a short questioning
phrase.*] No, no . . . I didn't mean that . . . I know very well that
mothers always talk nonsense when it comes to their children,
but even Rosetta, my sister Rosetta I mean, whom you perhaps
know because she's employed in your firm as a bookkeeper . . .
[*The saxophone, having calmed down, smoothly intones a short varia-
tion.*] Oh yes, yes, . . . Rosetta is a very good girl, just imagine,
she won't even dance with the guy she's engaged to marry. [*The
saxophone interrupts with an unfinished exclamation followed by two or
three questioning notes.*] The guy . . . the guy she's engaged to

marry, yes . . . He's a fine young man, believe me . . . he's in watches, he's a representative for a Swiss firm. [*The saxophone sneers.*] Well . . . it's as good as any job . . . Anyway, after they're married . . . [*The saxophone interrupts with short, raucous variations.*] But I didn't say they are getting married for sure. The plans are still indefinite . . . and, besides, my sister is so young. The important thing, for me, would be to show my mother that I'm working, and who knows, maybe one of these days my father will even decide to come back home. Oh, sir, if I could just . . . [*The saxophone interrupts with short, procrastinating little toots.*] Correct, quite correct . . . one shouldn't have meek eyes . . . I promise you I'll learn shorthand and typing and cultivate sharp, cunning glances. Give me a chance to prove it, sir . . . Please. [*While the* Boy *exits to the right, his words and the notes of the saxophone blend into a murmuring that fades away offstage.*]

Max. [*Not the slightest bit curious.*] Who are those two?

Jack. A boy . . . who lives outside.

Max. Outside the forest?

Jack. No, outside, in his own world . . . He's suffered a lot because of his family, so he's created a life all his own; he goes around reciting it to himself.

Max. That boy?

Jack. Yes, he's a poet. He wanted his father to quit playing roulette . . . his mother to change her way of life . . . his sister . . .

Max. [*Interrupting.*] Okay, but why is he talking to that gentleman?

Jack. He talks to all of them, to the gentleman, to his mother, to his sister. But he lives outside and can't get free of his past . . . We can barely get two words out of him. He'll listen, answer with a word or two, then suddenly run away. Oh, if you only knew how much the vinedresser's done to tame him . . . Yeah, but you don't know the vinedresser, so why bother?

Max. [*After pondering a moment.*] Well, this is none of our business.

Jack. Just what I was going to say. And besides, if you had to keep track of everybody living in the forest . . . The general, for instance, thinks of nothing but his machines.

Max. [*Showing his annoyance.*] No, I'm not interested in generals.

Jack. [*Bringing out a pair of large, shiny jackboots from behind the pump.*] Just look at these boots . . . nice, aren't they? And yet he doesn't want them.

Max. He doesn't want them?

Jack. No, he insists on wearing slippers.

Max. [*Nervously.*] Your general doesn't interest me. [*Pause.*] You do, though . . . you were talking about getting farther and farther away. Finally . . . [*insinuating*] finally you ended up a prisoner of your gasoline pump.

Jack. A prisoner? Not at all. [*Pause, then cautiously.*] What about you? How did you lose your way?

Max. [*Giving a start.*] Who said I lost my way? [*Brusquely.*] We're tourists . . . campers . . .

Jack. We? Who?

Max. [*Pointing to the tent.*] Me and Margot . . . Margot's still sleeping.

Jack. You both arrived last night? Where's your boat?

Max. What do you mean, boat? We came on foot . . . walking during the night, when it's cool. We've always done that. We even set up camp after dark, and in the morning we wake up to the singing of the birds and take a look around us. [*Slowly and as if daydreaming.*] First the wonder of being alive . . . then the surprises of the countryside . . . The trembling of a branch in bloom, the slimy emerald green of a frog leaping around among the rocks . . . [*To* Jack, *with a mocking tone.*] Poetic, isn't it?

Jack. [*Admiringly.*] Gosh!

Max. This morning, for instance, I woke up to the singing of a nightingale.

Jack. That was me.

Max. You can imitate a nightingale's warble?

Jack. Also the blackbird's whistle, the crow's caw, the thrush's song . . . I don't mean to brag, but I've gotten pretty good. In fact, every now and then the birds flying by will swoop down and answer me back. Then, of course, they catch on to the trick and fly off.

Max. Why do they catch on?

Jack. Probably because I don't know how to give the right answer. I do imitations, but I don't know their language. For all I know they could be asking me, "What's it like living in this forest? Are there any tasty worms? Are there any hunters . . . any traps?" And I answer back: "Six times seven is forty-two" or some other nonsense. And they fly off.

Max. I like your pastimes. Do you have any others?

Jack. No, sir. When I was in the city and could read the newspapers, I always read the crime reports.

Max. Why?

Jack. I liked to correct the mistakes of the murderers. "He split his rival's head open with a hatchet blow and was immediately arrested . . ." Why his rival's? He should have known that by killing his rival he would get caught right away. If he'd split open the head of the first person he ran into . . . Isn't that right? Don't you agree?

Max. Sure. [*Pause, then offering him some money.*] Would you mind warbling something? [*Pointing to the tent.*] To play a joke on Margot . . . I'd like her to think she's having a romantic awakening.

Jack. [*Heading toward the tent.*] Redbreast? Blackcap? Turtledove?

Max. Let's make it two turtledoves . . . two turtledoves billing and cooing.

Jack. That's not the problem . . . what can I say? . . . I wouldn't ever want to wake up anyone who was asleep. This Margot, for instance . . . What if she's dreaming she's free and happy, and we pull her back down to earth?

Max. [*Brusquely.*] What nonsense! Sooner or later she'll wake up anyway.

Jack. Okay, come on. [*He approaches the tent and shapes his hands into a funnel in front of his lips; in the wings a flute, alternating back and forth between two notes, imitates the cooing of turtledoves. Margot, a woman of about thirty, comes out of the tent scantily clad and stretches her arms. She is the embodiment of the cinematographic idea of the femme fatale: pale face, puckered blood-red lips, heavily made-up eyes, flaming red hair.*]

Margot. Hi, Max . . . what a sleep! I dreamed I was in a forest and two turtledoves were cooing up in a tree.

Max. [*Laughing.*] When you sleep, you get so idyllic . . . but for once that's really the case. Last night we set up camp in a forest.

Margot. [*Yawning and looking around.*] Really? It's fabulous!

Max. [*To Jack, who is dazzled at the sight of the woman.*] Do you like her?

Jack. Gosh! It's like she's in technicolor.

Max. [*Frivolously.*] That's how I wanted her . . . bewitching, dazzling. [*As if to himself.*] Cars and women in flashy colors. [*To Jack.*] Capricious, vivacious, unpredictable.

Jack. You're lucky to have such a woman. [*He continues looking at the woman, then with a sigh.*] Well, if you'll excuse me. [*He goes over to one of the bits of metallic debris and starts making quick, regular blows on it with a small steel bar. After a while another metallic sound answers him in the distance, and another still farther off.*]

Margot. What's that he's doing?

Max. [*To Jack.*] Hey! What is it? Your tom-tom?

Jack. [*Returning to the gasoline pump.*] I *do* have to announce your arrival.

Max. Thanks, but we won't be staying here long.

Jack. And where will you go?

Max. [*Flying into a rage.*] Oh brother! Wherever we please. Do we need somebody's permission?

Margot. Don't lose your temper, Max; let's start looking for mushrooms instead.

Max. Mushrooms?

Margot. [*Innocently.*] Yes, mushrooms. What do you expect to do in a forest? [*To* Jack.] Are there any mushrooms around here?

Jack. I've never seen any, but you might find some tin cans that used to have mushrooms in them. [*He rummages around in the weeds, picks up a tin can and holds it out to Margot.*] Here.

Margot. [*Sniffing the rusty tin can.*] You can't smell anything. [*Observing more closely.*] Oh yeah, small mushrooms in oil . . . That's what it says.

Max. [*To* Margot, *pointing to* Jack.] Do you know he witnessed the birth of the forest?

Margot. [*Absentmindedly.*]: No, really?!

Max. Isn't that something? . . . What's more, he has friends. Even a general.

Margot. [*To* Jack, *in an affected voice.*] I do hope you'll introduce him to us.

Jack. Sure. [*Looking toward the back.*] And here's the Professor. He's always one of the first to hear the signal. [*Waving his arm.*] Hello, Professor . . . [*In the distance appears a thin, emaciated, ragged figure with a knapsack over his shoulder; as he comes forward, every now and then he bends over to pick up something.*]

Professor. Good morning, everyone.

Max. [*To* Jack.] Is he a beggar?

Professor. [*Who has obviously overheard.*] No, I'm not looking for handouts. [*He picks up a tin can and puts it to his ear.*] Did you arrive last night?

Jack. Yes, last night. They're campers.

Margot. [*Laughing.*] But what are you listening to? That's not a seashell, you know.

Professor. It's all the same. Besides, there aren't any seashells around here. [*Holding the tin can out to* Margot.] Try it.

Margot. [*Putting the tin can to her ear.*] You're right, you do hear a humming.

Professor. [*Taking back the tin can and tossing it away.*] Maybe the humming of the machines that manufactured thousands of those little containers.

Margot. [*After a pause, and just to be polite.*] Do you live in the forest, too?

Professor. Well, since you can't get out of it . . .

Max. [*To* Margot, *with liveliness.*] That's just a manner of speaking. It means that you've become so used to it that you can't do without it. Like when someone says he can't get away from his business . . . They're just figures of speech.

Margot. [*Confused, observing the ragged man.*] Just figures of speech . . .

Professor. [*To* Max, *with just a hint of irony.*] You, on the other hand, are sure you can leave whenever you want.

Max. [*Shrugging his shoulders.*] All you have to do is keep walking straight in front of you. The forest can't be infinite . . . even space isn't infinite.

Professor. [*With a sigh.*] Because it's curved . . . but that's just speculation. Don't listen to the scientists.

Max. [*A little nervous.*] What did you do before you started going around masquerading in this way?

Professor. I masqueraded in a different way.

Jack. He was a professor . . . a professor at a university.

Professor. [*To* Max.] Don't be upset. Culture is a vainglorious sin, these rags are a vainglorious sin. [*Sneering.*] Man is a vainglorious animal.

Max. [*Muttering while closely observing the ragged man.*] Professor at a university. Well, I'll be! . . .

Margot. Man is a vainglorious and insecure animal.

Max. [*Smiling.*] She's referring to my passion for staying on the move. [*In the distance the beating of the tom-tom is heard again.*]

Margot. [*Dragging a rubber mattress out of the tent and stretching out on it.*] I, on the other hand, would never budge. If I could, I'd stay in a horizontal position all day long.

Max. [*To the* Professor.] Did you get the play on words? Horizontal . . . A position that can easily become a profession.

Margot. [*To the* Professor.] If they had their way, men would like to monopolize even dishonor. [*To* Max.] At least let us prostitute ourselves . . . it's one of our oldest prerogatives.

Professor. [*To* Max.] You said staying on the move. You meant, running away . . . Running away disguised as staying on the move, and fear following close behind you. [*Laughing ironically.*] Fear with its hooked hands . . .

Max. What do I have to be afraid of? [*He makes an attempt at laughing.*]

Professor. [*As if to himself.*] We all say that. What do we have to be afraid of? . . .

Jack. [*Staring into space.*] And yet, the fear is there. And we're all listening for something. [*In the distance is heard the mournful whistle of a train, followed by the rhythmic beating of a drum that fades away. Jack and the Professor look toward the back of the forest with visible worry, then slowly regain their composure in a heavy silence.*]

Max. [*Vaguely uneasy.*] What is it? [*And when no one answers him.*] Say something!

Margot. [*To the Professor, springing into a sitting position.*] Say something, please . . . Something . . . Even if you think it will insult me, but speak . . . speak . . . I think you were saying . . .

Professor. [*Distracted.*] I don't remember any more.

Max. [*With the same anxiety as Margot.*] We're all listening for something . . . yes, that's just what you were saying.

Professor. [*Goodheartedly.*] And then we realize that a seashell or a tin can give off the same humming sound.

Margot. [*Stretching out, appeased.*] Oh, wonderful!

Professor. [*Laughing ironically.*] The humming of our own ears.

Max. [*With a sigh of relief.*] Very good . . . go on.

Professor. The same thing happens with other voices. [*Listening.*] Who called me? [*Pause, then sadly.*] No one . . . It would be too beautiful, it would be a miracle. We all wait for it, but they are only internal voices, the gurglings of our imagination, acoustic illusions, hope that something will finally reach us from outside. [*Shaking his head.*] But nothing ever happens. From our birth to our death, nothing! [*The Boy reappears on the right, speaking in an upset and grieved tone. The invisible character answers him with chords from a cello. This time the Boy crosses the stage in the opposite direction, that is, from right to left.*]

Boy. Oh, no, Mama; try to be reasonable, it's not that I don't want to obey you, but I'm not qualified for that job. Besides, I don't know shorthand . . . I don't know anything about figures or business or accounts and invoices. They set horrible traps for my brain. [*The cello emits three notes that seem to be three negations, each at a different pitch.*] Don't you believe me? Why don't you ever believe anything I say? [*The cello repeats the three notes.*] Oh, Mama, how can I explain to you? Even that gentleman didn't seem enthusiastic to me . . . Yes, he was pleasant, but pleasant in a superficial and ambiguous way . . . [*The cello cautiously questions with a few chords.*] Spider's legs, that's it . . . jointed legs crawling slowly . . . [*Pause. One lone imperious note.*] No, I'm not just being silly, and I'm not imagining things either . . . On my skin, here . . . sticky tentacles.

[*Becoming progressively excited.*] Just try to understand me . . . I'm your son, I beg you. I can work in a thousand other ways . . . [*The cello executes a kind of short laugh.*] Leave my poems out of it . . . [*Flying into a rage.*] I'm tired of this merciless irony, this constant derision . . . It's . . . unkind. [*Trying to contain himself.*] It almost seems as though you and Rosetta are plotting against me, both of you . . . [*The cello softly executes some short variations.*] That's not true! Rosetta's not a baby anymore! [*Upset.*] And it's funny how I'm the one who has to make you notice certain things, I'm the one who has to draw attention to certain situations. [*Screaming.*] But why? Why are you trying to make me say things I don't want to? Why do you drive me to despair, both of you! Leaving me to wander around alone in the night like a distant comet . . . [*He puts his hands to his face, while the cello executes a series of wailing sobs.*] No, Mama, don't go away . . . I'll do what you say, I swear! [*Screaming as he dashes off after his hallucination.*] Mama, no . . . stop, Mama! [*His voice is lost offstage as are the cello's discordant notes that chase each other in a frenzied fugue.*]

Margot. [*Jumping to her feet and seized by violent excitement.*] Stop him! Stop him!

Max. [*Holding her back by her arm.*] What are you trying to do?

Margot. [*Restless.*] I want to talk to him . . . I have to talk to him.

Max. [*Fuming with anger.*] Oh, this damned flair of yours for the melodramatic! Won't you ever get over it!

Margot. But he's just a boy, don't you see! Just a boy.

Max. [*Drawing away.*] I get it . . . you're attracted to him.

Margot. [*Trembling.*] Will you cut it out? [*To the* Professor.] You know what's wrong. Tell me, why are they tormenting him? Why is everyone against him?

Professor. [*Shrugging his shoulders.*] It's not that everyone's against him, it's life that's against everyone. [*As if speaking to himself.*] Life . . . Why should he be an exception?

Margot. [*To* Jack.] His sister, this Rosetta . . .

Jack. [*With indifference.*] She's the gentleman's mistress.

Margot. Was it her mother's doing?

Professor. Yes, she needs money to keep her husband from running off. She's jealous of her husband.

Margot. I don't get it.

Jack. Her husband's a gambler. He's always needing money and so he cashes in on his wife's jealousy.

Professor. [*To* Margot.] You know what a gambler is . . . All he sees is the roulette wheel, the numerical cycles, the repetitions, the doublings . . . He probably has his own martingale, his own system . . . he doesn't care about anything else. [*As if to himself.*] Just him and chance, like two wrestlers.

Margot. [*Bewildered.*] He doesn't even care about his own son?

Max. [*Snorting.*] Now she's hot for the gambler! Life does nothing but imitate the movies.

Margot. [*Flying into a rage.*] You're disgusting! [*Forlornly repeating her earlier words.*] Not even about his own son . . .

Professor. He's a useless being.

Margot. Useless? Why?

Professor. He's an aesthete, a dreamer. And the more he struggles to escape from the spider web of his compromises, the more entangled he becomes . . . Besides, I think he enjoys it.

Jack. [*Goodheartedly.*] The lady is a newcomer to the forest . . . You'll get used to it.

Margot. [*Looking around frightened as if she were establishing a relation with the countryside.*] A spider web . . . and all of us are caught in it . . .

Max. [*Flying into a rage.*] What do you mean, all of us? I go where I please!

Professor. [*Sneering.*] Within the cage.

Max. [*Irritable.*] That's fine with me! As long as it's wide, very wide! Wide enough to walk around in for miles . . . And who says it's not interesting as well? Watching the other caged people . . . yourself . . . [*No one has noticed that the* Vinedresser *has come forward from the back of the forest; he is a middle-aged man dressed like a peasant; his face and hands, because of their refined quality, contrast with his coarse clothes and his wooden shoes.*]

Vinedresser. [*Stopping a short distance from the tent.*] Good morning, everyone; forgive me for being late.

Jack. [*As if relieved.*] Oh, here's the vinedresser. Didn't you hear the signal?

Vinedresser. I was far away.

Professor. [*Sneering.*] Somewhere between a lost past and an uncertain future.

Vinedresser. And hope? Isn't that possibly a human feeling? And what justification would it have if it were not synonymous with salvation?

Jack. Please, don't start on that. [*Then, as a means of introduction.*] This lady and this gentleman arrived a little while ago . . . they're campers.

Max. [*Jovially.*] You're the vinedresser? That's good.

Vinedresser. Why?

Max. A vinedresser presupposes a vineyard. [*Laughing ironically.*] Cheer up, Margot . . . the time's come to open up chest B. [*To the* Professor.] All our luggage is labeled . . . A . . . B . . . C . . .

Professor. [*Filling in.*] . . . and in chest B . . . bottles!

Max. Exactly! [*The* Vinedresser *has drawn near the tent and timidly feels the texture as if evaluating its worth.*]

Margot. Do you like it? It's a special fabric, durable and waterproof. Max is very proud of it.

Vinedresser. Silk?

Max. Silk, indeed! It's a new blend with a synthetic resin base. After the Stone Age and the Iron Age, we've now arrived at the Synthetic Resin Age.

Vinedresser. [*Still feeling the tent.*] Touching it gives a sensation that's . . .

Professor. [*Finishing his sentence.*] . . . repulsive.

Max. Why?

Professor. It's not cloth, it's not leather, it's not rubber. It's not vegetable, it's not mineral. It doesn't belong to any of the realms of nature to which we were accustomed, and therefore our epidermis receives a somewhat loathsome sensation from it.

Max. [*Annoyed.*] I already said it's a synthetic resin.

Professor. Exactly . . . algebraic formulas glued together . . . hydrogen and nitrogen made viscous . . . gas that's been compressed and laminated or cast into molds. Out of it you can make transparent drinking glasses that aren't glass, buttons that aren't bone, tents that aren't cloth . . .

Max. Still, this is a fabric.

Professor. Out of which you'll never make a flag, or a blanket, or a shroud.

Max. All I care about is being protected from the dampness of the night.

Vinedresser. Do you always take it with you?

Max. Always.

Vinedresser. Constantly traveling?

Max. Constantly traveling.

Vinedresser. And not one place in the world to go back to in order to collect yourself?

Max. Not one place in the world.

Margot. [*With goodhearted resignation.*] We travel around like snails, with our house on our backs.

Vinedresser. But snails were born that way.

Margot. And that's how we've become.

Max. [*Clapping his hands.*] Margot . . . the bottles!

Margot. [*She goes to the tent and comes back carrying a small chest. She opens it and takes out some bottles and glasses. To* Max.] Whisky?

Max. Naturally. [*He opens a bottle and begins to pour, then as he offers drinks to the others.*] The glasses are made out of plexiglass, but the whisky is genuine. [*Everyone takes a glass, halfheartedly expressing his or her gratitude.*]

Vinedresser. Industry today makes it possible to solve many problems. [*Indicating the tent.*] If someone doesn't have a permanent shelter, he gets one that's movable and carries it around with him.

Margot. [*Laughing.*] Don't get Max started on that tent. He's convinced it can withstand any storm whatsoever. As for me, I've known war; I'm less optimistic when it comes to tents.

Max. [*Goodheartedly.*] Aw . . . The Empire State Building is sturdier, but you can't go around with a skyscraper on your back.

Vinedresser. Do you believe the Empire State Building makes a safe shelter?

Max. It depends on what you want to use it for.

Vinedresser. I believe that there are no safe shelters.

Max. Not even faith?

Vinedresser. Why do you ask me that?

Max. Come off it! Vinedresser . . . an easy enough riddle. The vineyards of the Lord, the vintage; the wine that turns to blood . . . The ancient symbolism that crops up from the catacombs like a weed.

Professor. [*To* Jack.] Speaking of cropping up . . . did you see that an arm has sprung up down there? [*He points toward the back of the forest.*]

Jack. I saw . . . Yesterday the wind was making the fingers of the hand move like it was waving.

Margot. A woman's arm?

Jack. I don't know. A skeleton's arm was all I could tell . . .

Max. [*As if to himself.*] Sometimes the dead get tired of waiting and make signs . . . [*Pause; then rousing himself,* Max *says to the* Vinedresser.] But you still haven't answered my question.

Vinedresser. [*Wearily.*] Why all this curiosity?

Max. Curiosity is the best way to call attention to oneself, and I am the prototype for individualism.

Vinedresser. As opposed to the multitude?

Max. Especially! [*Gulping down what is left in his glass and pouring himself some more liquor.*] But you call them brothers!

Vinedresser. [*Wearily.*] I've lived with the masses, and I don't regret what my heart has suffered.

Max. [*Ironically, while he goes around pouring for the others.*] The bleeding heart beneath the overalls. Mass celebrated in the factories and in the mines . . . It's an experiment you shouldn't have been trying to make.

Vinedresser. It was an order, and I followed it.

Max. But you didn't follow the counterorder.

Vinedresser. I followed the counterorder as well.

Max. And that's why you are in the forest. Well then, I'll repeat the question for you . . . What about faith?

Vinedresser. [*Flying into a rage.*] It's still there, yes, it's still there! [*He looks anxiously toward the sky, then lowering his voice.*] Assuming that it's permissible to call attention to the fact.

Max. Shaken by a thousand doubts . . .

Vinedresser. Not one single doubt . . . anxiety maybe . . . anguish because of the quest for truth. [*As if to himself.*] Even the Apostles doubted.

Max. And when did this bewilderment begin? [*From this moment on the light begins gradually to dim while violent gusts of wind are heard accompanied by light strokes on a violin.*]

Vinedresser. I don't know . . . [*As if to himself.*] A kind of disease . . . Who can say when a disease starts? When it reveals itself, it's almost always too late.

Jack. [*Looking upward.*] I told you so . . . The wind's changed.

Max. [*Ironically.*] And the storm's coming.

Jack. Sometimes everything gets dark, a kind of artificial night.

Max. Let's welcome even the artificial night.

Margot. [*Lifting her glass.*] What'll we drink to?

Professor. Usually we drink to what we don't have.

Max. Well then, let's drink to immortality. [*Nodding toward the Vinedresser.*] He's the only one who believes in it.

Professor. To avoid arguments, let's drink to some other abstraction . . . to glory, for instance. [*Laughing.*] It presents just as many problems as immortality.

Max. [*Lifting his glass.*]

> ". . . a circle in the water,
> Which never ceaseth to enlarge itself
> Till by broad spreading it disperse to nought."

Professor. Pay no attention to Shakespeare; he was a sucker for glory, too. [*There is again heard the distant mournful whistle of the train.* Jack, *the* Professor, *and the* Vinedresser *turn toward the back of the stage. Their faces express an apprehension bordering on fear.*]

Max. Is there a train in the forest?

Jack. [*Vexed.*] No. There's no train.

Max. Yet this is the second time I thought I heard . . .

Professor. [*With a sigh.*] The lament, my good sir . . . merely the lament of a train.

Max. What a shame . . . a train could settle everything.

Jack. [*Flying into a rage.*] That's what he's always saying. [*He points to the* Professor.] But I'd just like to see him face to face with it, I'd just like to see him . . . [*He tries to restrain his unexpected emotion.*]

Professor. [*To* Max, *nodding toward* Jack.] The fear of the ignorant . . . the childish fear of the dark, of the leap into the void. [*Nodding toward the* Vinedresser.] A fear they've always exploited to their advantage.

Vinedresser. [*Sadly to* Max.] Do you hear him? We just can't understand each other.

Professor. That's why we're here. [*The gusts of wind increase; the light continues to dim.*]

Margot. [*Going into the tent and coming back out with a black cloak which she throws over her shoulders.*] Don't you feel how cold the air's gotten . . . and how humid.

Jack. It's always like that before a storm.

Max. [*He, too, makes for the tent.*] Do you want some covers? [*Bringing out some more black wraps similar to Margot's cloak.*] No more synthetic resins! These are made out of wool with the oil still on it . . . the shepherds of the island use them when the wind scours the mountain and the rain floods the valley. [*Handing out the covers to everyone.*] In such times the shepherds bundle themselves up in these wraps and stay put, squatting on the stony ground, like bats all wrapped up in their wings. [*They all take the funereal wraps and fall down in various positions all around the stage, over which has now fallen a violet-colored darkness broken by sulfurous flashes of lightning followed by the occasional roll of distant thunder. The similarity with the bats mentioned by Max becomes evident. Silence. Then* Jack, *who has curled up in his cloak near the gasoline pump, pulls out his harmonica and starts playing a sad dirge consisting of a few notes squeezed out to the rhythm of his breathing. An occasional pause; and then one of the cloaked figures comes out with a phrase that is a comment on and the conclusion of his own thoughts, as happens in the half-awake state of people wracked with fever.*]

Vinedresser. . . . lost road . . . and grace farther and farther off . . . help us, O Lord . . .

Professor. . . . impossible to construct the future . . . and even more difficult to abolish the past . . . Liberation, where are you? Why so much fear of death?

Max. . . . to speak a different language . . . pride and con-
demnation of the individual . . . All around, the emaciated
slaves lift their chains as they sing hosannas.
Margot. . . . lost sweetness . . . shadow and silence . . . and each
day I sink down . . . angels with burnt wings gaze upon me.
[Jack *starts up again with his sad music, then becomes silent.*]
Vinedresser. . . . bitter exile . . . painful night . . . and the Marys
weep on Calvary.
Professor. . . . Mother! Daughter! Why are you calling me? . . . Life
sinks down into a lake without moorings . . . The useless jour-
ney is about to end.
Max. . . . the dead with their eyes wide open . . . and the silence of
the white cell that haunts me . . .
Margot. . . . you tread on my heart without leaving marks, like
storks flying low over rice paddies with their coral legs barely
grazing the water.
[Jack *starts playing again; the wind becomes stronger, the darkness
becomes deeper, and the scrim slowly closes. While the scrim is closed,
with only the footlights dimly lit, the storm unleashes itself behind the
projection of the forest, amidst rolls of thunder, while a woodwind and
brass music rises to a tempestuous crescendo, interspersed with cries,
pleas, and moans. Then suddenly everything becomes quiet. And the
scrim opens up on the second scene.*]

SCENE 2

*A flash of yellowish light illuminates the forest of debris. The storm is over,
leaving a bewildered calm in the air. An occasional broken piece of debris
dangles, moved by the last gusts of wind. A telegraph pole has been
smashed. The campers' gear is haphazardly piled up under the rigging of
steel wire that held up the tent, which has been uprooted by the storm. The*
Vinedresser, *stretched out on his cloak, raises up with difficulty, supporting himself on one elbow.* Margot, *close by him, is trying to revive him by
pouring a couple of drops of liquor between his lips. The bodies and hair of
both are dripping wet.*

Margot. [*Speaking tenderly.*] Have a sip, Vinedresser . . . There's
nothing like this to settle your nerves.
Vinedresser. [*Pushing away the glass.*] No, that's enough. [*Pause.*]
Where did they go?
Margot. [*Trying to be cheerful.*] They all went running after the tent.
You should have seen the wind take it . . . it was like a big bird

with huge wings. And Max kept running and running, leaping like a deer . . .

Vinedresser. [*Like an echo.*] The tent . . .

Margot. [*Clinging to the neck of the bottle.*] You really should have some . . . this is liquid dynamite. Max may have his faults, but he knows his whisky. [*Laughing.*] So do I . . . I didn't serve with the legionnaires in the war for nothing.

Vinedresser. With the legionnaires?

Margot. Seventh battalion of the Second Foreign Regiment.

Vinedresser. [*Getting to his feet with difficulty.*] You were saying that Max . . .

Margot. That he knows his whisky. [*As if to herself.*] But it isn't the alcohol that's poisoned him. [*Tapping her forehead with her finger.*] A thought gnaws at him . . . here.

Vinedresser. And you love him? Why?

Margot. I don't know . . . When I met him, he had a shock of hair that fell down on his forehead . . . laughing eyes. [*Gulping down another swallow.*] Frivolity, huh? No! Intelligence and mystery of nature. [*Laughing ironically, somewhat drunk.*] And he clung to me, too, because of an illusion . . . It happens, doesn't it? There comes a time in your life when you would like to believe in everything . . . to have faith in every single thing.

Vinedresser. You hope and you fear.

Margot. You are afraid of being alone . . . in the midst of people who can't understand—which is worse than being alone . . . Pride, too, at feeling yourself cursed . . . That's it, pride and fear.

Vinedresser. [*As if to himself.*] I don't hear anything but that word. Fear!

Margot. [*As if to herself.*] Three months in a white cell, lighted night and day by a huge electric light, and not a soul spoke to him. They gave him his food through a hole in the door . . . Not moving for three months, in the white silence of a cell, without being able to speak . . . He finally went crazy!

Vinedresser. [*Giving a start.*] Max?

Margot. Yes . . . that was what they wanted . . . The only way to force a name and an address out of his mouth. [*She drinks another long swallow.*] And so the other guy was seized and put before a firing squad. His closest friend . . . almost a brother . . . [*As if to herself.*] Then the running away started . . .

Vinedresser. Was he afraid of losing his life?

Margot. He was afraid of the other guy's money. The other guy had made out his will to him, and Max, who didn't know that, was horrified at the money. [*With a sudden change of tone.*] Nice, huh? It's like a novel . . . [*Back to her former tone.*] And then he was on the run with the tent, the bottles, the portable radio. [*Laughing ironically.*] A fear of silence . . . When I'm asleep, he plays the radio, or else goes looking for the first person passing by, just to hear somebody talk . . . talk . . . talk . . . Then we pack up our gear and we're off . . . from one city to the next, from one continent to the next; with the tent, the pots, the bottles . . . [*Takes another drink.*] Me and the bottles, we're certainly the most useful objects.

Vinedresser. You're not an object, you're a human being.

Margot. [*Laughing ironically.*] What's that supposed to mean? My father, too, was a human being . . . so was my mother.

Vinedresser. Where are they?

Margot. I didn't know my mother. I was born and she died . . . They burned my father with a shower of napalm . . . do you know what napalm is? That stuff the airplanes drop down . . . liquid fire. [*She drinks with one gulp what is left in the bottle.*] That's what it is, liquid fire . . .

Vinedresser. In war?

Margot. [*Sitting down heavily.*] Let's say guerrilla warfare. In the Orient, where my father was a political exile. I'm the daughter of peasants . . . Marguerite Leonnèc . . . a Breton family name, people who have farmed all their life in the Landes . . . hardy stock . . . [*Pause.*] My father made me study to be a schoolteacher. [*Laughing ironically.*] Schoolteacher . . . funny, isn't it? Then the war comes along. Pow! pow! pow! [*A peal of thunder resounds like an echo.*] See, like that! Only louder . . . and we become rebels. [*Pause.*] Don't you get it? [*Throwing the bottle away.*] In wartime anybody who doesn't submit to the occupying troops automatically becomes a rebel . . . And that's why they burned the village . . . I escaped by hiding in the rice paddies. [*Pause.*] Then the legionnaires came along and pulled me out by one of my legs like a frog. [*She gets up, totally drunk, and from this moment on her story, interspersed with peals of thunder, voices, and music, becomes the raving of a drunken woman fighting with her ghosts. The voices and the bits of music will, as usual, be transmitted by the loudspeakers placed about the theater.* Margot *resumes, reeling about as she walks.*] Trial for espionage . . . an excuse . . . they knew perfectly well I couldn't have been a spy.

A Voice. [*Imperiously.*] What is your name?

Margot. Marguerite Leonnèc, daughter of the late Sebastien . . .

The Same Voice. Why did you hide from the liberating troops?

Margot. [*Laughing ironically.*] Do you think it was fun remaining out in the open? [*To the* Vinedresser, *with a change of tone.*] In the end they had to acquit me, and they sent me to a concentration camp along with the native women . . . Barbed wire and hunger to your heart's content . . . [*Speaking to herself.*] So much hunger! And only one way to get food . . . do you understand, Vinedresser? Only one way.

Vinedresser. I don't want to know any more.

Margot. [*Like an annoyed child.*] Oh, yes, you must know . . . those barracks with red lights, for instance, didn't you ever hear of them? Barracks with cubicles. In each cubicle a bed and a woman. [*With her voice somewhat mellow.*] Every twenty-four hours a distribution of food from the noncommissioned officers' mess . . . a medical checkup once a week, and during transfers we traveled on trucks rigged up with benches. [*Pause, then as if dreaming.*] The war continued and I continued to . . . how can I put it elegantly? Oh, yes . . . I continued to busy myself with the physiological equilibrium of the troops . . . [*Laughing.*] Yes, that's the wording of the army regulations. Physiological equilibrium of the troops . . . To complain about it would have been defeatism. [*Far off are heard sounds of shooting that become more intense, mixed with the voices of those fighting. Only* Margot *listens to this aural hallucination.*]

Voices. [*Far off and confused.*] Long live the Legion . . . Fire! The Legion does not surrender! First gun fire! . . . Second gun fire! . . . Third gun . . . [*A distant bugle sounds the charge.*]

Margot. [*Gleefully.*] Do you hear them, Vinedresser? It's the entrenched camp at Tein-fu . . . Seventeen hundred men in a trap . . . [*Sneering.*] The Chinese are attacking like ants . . . the food supplies are all used up . . . there's no more water, we have to surrender. [*Changing her tone.*] Now comes the good part. There's a whole big ceremony . . . The flag buried so it won't fall into the hands of the rebels . . . [*There is heard the roar of an airplane taking off and flying away.*] Do you hear that? The camp commander has sent the nurses off to safety in the last airplane left. Three very good nurses, who took care of the wounded under fire . . . [*From time to time one still hears the roar of the plane flying away.*] There they go . . . the nurses have left, they are far away, flying toward Europe . . . [*Looking around, terrified.*] And now? There's nothing left to do now but raise a scrap of white cloth. [*Becoming louder.*] And the Chinese will be here . . . the yellow men . . . the ones who cut women's throats with the hooks of their bamboo cutters. [*Screaming desperately.*] Commander, Commander, you can't do this! . . . I'm a European!

. . . I'm a Frenchwoman! [*With a very shrill scream, she covers her face with her hands.*]

Vinedresser. [*Jumping up and supporting the tottering woman.*] Calm down, for the love of God! You've drunk too much.

Margot. [*Gently freeing herself.*] Don't worry, Vinedresser. Drunkenness passes quickly . . . and then the war was over. [*The loudspeakers in the orchestra pit emit a sound of distant music. Voices sing the "Marseillaise" while faint rounds of applause break through.*] Listen! Vinedresser! It's the crowd welcoming the veterans . . . Flowers, medals, music . . . The Croix de Guerre for the heroic nurses. [*Singing softly.*] Allons enfants de la Patrie, le jour de gloire est arrivé . . .

A Voice. [*Closer, of a policeman.*] Get back! Get back! Keep the street clear for the parade . . . [*The "Marseillaise" becomes louder but always remaining in the background while the applause becomes deafening.*]

Margot. [*Nudging with her elbows as if she were crushed by the crowd.*] Just a minute! Let me through . . . Let me through, I said! I want a decoration, too . . . [*More and more excitedly.*] A diploma for being a first-class whore . . . Mr. President, listen to me! I did my duty . . . the physiological equilibrium of the troops . . . [*A peal of thunder followed by a heavy silence.* Margot *has collapsed on the ground and is laughing softly, as if tired of an exhausting game.*]

Vinedresser. [*Kneeling down next to the woman.*] Please, in the name of God, calm down.

Margot. [*Getting up halfway, but remaining on her knees and numbed by her drunkenness, which is beginning to disappear.*] In the name of God? Okay, but we'd need a miracle.

Vinedresser. To receive a miracle you have to believe.

Margot. What I'm waiting for is too great.

Vinedresser. There is no wish that God cannot fulfill.

Margot. [*Starting to babble again.*] The man dressed in red . . .

Vinedresser. Don't start up again, for pity's sake . . .

Margot. [*Delirious.*] The man dressed in red ought to come back, with His lean face, shiny with sweat and blood, with the crown of thorns . . . He'd understand me . . . If He returned to look at us with His shining eyes, we would all kneel down . . .

Vinedresser. [*Fervently.*] But He died on the Cross precisely for our salvation, and then He arose . . .

Margot. [*With a gesture of annoyance.*] No . . . you bungled everything . . . why didn't you leave Him to us as He was? Poor, worn-out, like we are . . .

Vinedresser. [*Going away.*] I can't listen to you any more.

Margot. [*Stretching out a hand in a timid caress.*] Don't go away . . .

[*Smiling sadly.*] I'm the first woman who's talked to you like this since your mother, aren't I? [*Reflecting.*] Yes, that must be how it is . . . You came to this desert from a greater solitude . . .

Vinedresser. A solitude offered to God.

Margot. [*Rising with difficulty.*] And why should God demand an inhuman sacrifice of you, since he created you as a man?

Vinedresser. I said offered, I didn't say it was demanded of me. Why can't you understand this, you who have suffered, too? You who have such impulses of generosity?

Margot. [*Trying to take her first steps without reeling.*] What impulses?

Vinedresser. The Boy, for instance . . . See . . . you were filled with pity for that poor boy.

Margot. [*As if struck by an unexpected memory.*] Oh, yeah, the Boy . . . Can't anything be done for him? [*Excitedly.*] I must speak to him . . . I have to try . . . maybe fate wanted to offer me this last chance, a lifeline . . . something good at last. [Max *appears from the back, dragging the tattered tent.* Jack *and the* Professor *follow him, holding up the other end of the tent.*]

Max. We got it! [*Stopping to observe* Margot.] Hey? What are you doing? Are you saying your confession or arguing?

Margot. [*With a tired voice.*] Did you find the tent?

Max. [*Throwing it down with anger.*] A useless rag! And we had to chase it almost as far as the river.

Professor. [*Laughing ironically.*] Collapse of the synthetic resins. [*To* Max.] Keep calm, we'll mend it somehow . . . I'm a master of repairs.

Max. [*As if to himself.*] All we do is patch things up . . . We break crockery, then try to repair it. [*To the* Vinedresser *in an ironic tone, winking toward* Margot.] Did you try to convert her?

Vinedresser. I don't think there's any need. And besides, my powers are limited.

Max. [*In a falsely indifferent tone.*] What did you two talk about, then?

Margot. [*With a defiant voice.*] If you must know, we were talking about the Boy . . .

Max. Ah . . . the one that lives in the stratosphere? [*Pause.*] Does he interest you? [*To the* Vinedresser.] The mature and experienced woman, and the handsome and timid young man . . . [*Laughing.*] This is going to be awful.

Margot. [*Contemptuous.*] You get intoxicated from your own babble.

Max. Everybody gets drunk in their own way. But you're afraid of my babbling. [*At this moment the* Boy *appears among the trees but stops, intimidated.*]

Professor. [*To the* Boy.] Come on, come on . . . They won't eat you. [*To* Max.] Occasionally, he'll speak with us, but he's afraid of strangers.

Max. [*Turning around to look at him.*] Strangers? We aren't strangers anymore. We're bushmen, too . . . [*To the* Boy, *with a welcoming gesture.*] Come on down, nobody wants to eat you up. . . . How old are you? [*The* Boy *does not answer.*]

Jack. The gentleman asked you how old you are.

Boy. Twenty-four.

Max. [*To* Margot.] Twenty-four years old, just think! A load of vitality that probably will last another fifty years. [*Laughing.*] Twenty-four years old . . . When he passes by, women turn around as if they'd been touched by fire, and he walks on, oblivious, his body flaming with muscles and bones . . . He wanders away, enveloped in a thick cloud, like a pagan divinity. Mysterious and fascinating, like a gift of nature . . .

Margot. [*With her teeth clenched.*] I wish he'd slug you . . . slug you right in the nose!

Max. [*Goodheartedly drawing near to the* Boy.] That wouldn't be hard for him. He's got strong arms, and surely his reflexes are quicker than mine. But he won't do it. He's a poet. [*To* Margot.] A poet looking for a job. [*Laughing.*] Because even poets have to eat every day. [*To the* Boy.] This, you see, is one of the many imperfections of Creation. A handsome young man is born with the heart of a poet, but with a stomach that has to be filled three times a day.

Margot. [*Advancing resolutely.*] Leave him alone! [*To the* Boy.] Do you want to talk with me? Can we do anything to help you?

Boy. [*Timidly.*] Thank you . . . I'm not looking for help . . . I'm going to work so my mother and my sister won't need that gentleman . . . And my father, too, will come back home . . . then I'll be happy, and I'll go back to being at peace with myself.

Margot. [*Looking with anguish at the* Professor.] Who's to blame for this?

Professor. [*Shrugging his shoulders.*] No one's to blame. It's one of the cogs in the machine. Do you suppose you can put one of the cogs on trial? Establish precisely the responsibility of every little wheel?

Margot. [*To the* Boy.] Why don't you go somewhere far away? [*Smiling.*] You have a sailor's sweater . . .

Boy. [*Smiling at the woman.*] Sailor? Yes, I'd like that . . . I've tried, too, but it's not easy.

Margot. You tried to get on a ship?

Boy. Yes.

Margot. On a real ship?

Boy. [*Enthusiastic.*] Yes, a real one . . . with smoke, flags, whistles, the smell of tar, the name in gold letters on the stern . . . Oceania . . . Saturnia . . . and gulls flying all around, seesawing on their big wings . . .

Margot. And they didn't take you on?

Boy. [*A little sad.*] No. There's always someone else more capable, luckier maybe, who gets on board in my place. I don't know how it happens . . . Look, I know very well what I'm supposed to say . . . Do you want me to prove it? Watch . . . [*With the gestures and tone of an amateur preoccupied with reciting a small part that has been rehearsed a few times.*] Good morning, Captain . . . Forgive me for being so bold . . . [*Correcting himself.*] No, not like that . . . Good morning, Captain . . . [*With an outburst of crazed desperation.*] No, it's no good! I've tried these empty sentences too many times! [*He turns his back, puts his hands to his face as if he were about to burst into tears, then pulls himself together, but without turning around.*] I'm not crying in the slightest . . . I'm laughing instead. [*He laughs unconvincingly.*] See, I'm laughing . . . [*As he goes off, he laughs louder and louder, while he keeps repeating like a phonograph.*] Good morning Captain, good morning Captain, good morning Captain . . . [*This continues until it fades, along with his crazed laughter, into the background of the forest. Pause. The characters have remained motionless, with their eyes lowered, almost ashamed of themselves. In the distance the weak whistle of the train is heard again, followed by the beating of the drum, which is drawing closer. The beats are rhythmic and alternate with small rolls, like the kind used in funerals when the music stops.* Jack, *the* Professor, *and even the* Vinedresser, *all seized by a kind of panic, run back and forth as though seeking a means of escape, while the beating of the drum comes closer. When the drum stops, the* Conductor *appears from the back. He is a lean sort, dressed in dark clothing, with a bony face vaguely reminiscent of a skull. He has a black cap with the silver braiding of railway personnel; in his hand he holds a small ticket punch.*]

Conductor. [*Touching two fingers to his visor.*] Tickets, please. [*Everyone starts rummaging around in their pockets.* Max *and* Margot *go to look for their tickets in their gear.*]

Jack. [*Going up to the* Conductor *and holding out his ticket to him.*] Here it is. [*The* Conductor *examines it, punches it, and returns it to* Jack, *who goes back to his gasoline pump, obviously satisfied. The others also find their tickets, and one by one give them to the* Conductor. *The scene already enacted with* Jack *is repeated with bureaucratic precision.*

The only one left aside is the Professor, *who keeps looking through all his pockets and through the knapsack he has over his shoulder for his not-to-be-found ticket, while a more and more evident anxiety is shown on his face. The* Conductor, *who for some time has been eyeing the ragged figure over the tops of his glasses, slowly goes up to him while the other characters draw away, forming a large circle in order to observe the scene.*]

Conductor. [*With pretended good nature.*] Well then?

Professor. Just a moment . . . let me look . . . I'm sure I've got it right here. [*Removing his hat and rummaging through the band and inner lining.*] Where did I put it? That's the problem . . . where could I have put that damned ticket?

Conductor. [*In a vaguely distracted tone.*] It's no use.

Professor. I'm sorry, what did you say?

Conductor. I said it's no use. Your ticket's no good anymore.

Professor. [*Trying to appear nonchalant.*] What do you mean it's no good anymore? [*To the others with an ironic smile.*] He's jumping the gun . . . it's no good anymore . . . And anyway I'm sure I've got it.

Conductor. Yes, but it's expired.

Professor. Expired?

Conductor. Your ride's over.

Professor. [*Flying into a rage.*] What are you feeding me? [*He goes back to rummaging through all his pockets.*] Now, let's see . . . the date it was issued has to be on the ticket, doesn't it?

Conductor. You're telling *me,* who has punched holes in it all these years? I've been checking your ticket for sixty-five years, and the other times you always found it. Remember? You found it easily . . . Doesn't that suggest anything to you?

Professor. [*A little troubled.*] What's sixty-five years supposed to mean? A flash! An instant! I assure you I hardly noticed them.

Conductor. [*Goodheartedly.*] That's what they all say.

Professor. [*Remaining motionless with his arms hanging at his sides.*] So, you'd like to put me in a fix? Worse still, take every hope from me?

Conductor. [*Shrugging his shoulders.*] I don't know what hopes you might have . . . All I'm saying is that your ride's over.

Professor. But . . . but I know people who keep riding when they are seventy, even eighty years old . . . and then my family was always long-lived . . . I've never been sick . . . It's absolutely illogical that . . .

Max. [*With a sigh.*] Professor . . . why illogical? As a philosopher, you ought to know . . .

Professor. [*Flying into a rage.*] Go to hell! And don't bother me!

Max. Yet I remember when little Shanzer died, do you remember? The red-haired student who was in the third desk and used to cough all the time? [*Laughing.*] Oh, yeah . . . I didn't tell you I was one of your pupils. Of course, you don't remember me. But I still see you at the lectern, with your jacket a little threadbare at the elbows . . . I still hear your pompous, nasal voice, when you used to speak to us about death, about life, about eternity . . .

Professor. [*Shuddering.*] Listen, right now let me discuss things with the conductor. [*To the* Conductor.] There must be a misunderstanding here. [*Bursting out at* Max.] And besides, death is a personal matter, that's what it is . . . You can't criticize it in other people . . . Each person reacts to it differently.

Max. [*As if he had not heard.*] When the red-headed student died, you quoted Seneca. [*In a comically pompous tone.*] "Non est res magna vivere, omnes servi tui vivunt" et cetera, et cetera.

Professor. [*In another outburst.*] That will do! And so what? That's why I gave up teaching, because I realized that all the wisdom of the philosophers has never been of use for anything!

Max. [*Laughing ironically.*] Ha . . . Ha . . . Ha . . . Professor . . . We can give Seneca a little bit of credit; he was consistent, he cut his wrists.

Conductor. [*Annoyed.*] Listen . . . I don't have time to waste with these little tales.

Max. [*Laughing.*] Little tales . . . you're right!

Professor. [*To* Max, *furiously.*] Little tales, huh? That's fine and good for you, looking at it from the outside.

Max. Look at it from wherever you want . . . death is a pure fact, like birth. Precisely two facts that come to us from the outside, two identical phenomena.

Conductor. Shall we start over?

Professor. [*More and more exasperated.*] Give me some time to think! One minute more or less won't matter . . . And then, I have to finish my book . . . I'm writing a work of tremendous importance.

Max. [*Bursting out laughing.*] A work of tremendous importance! Ha . . . ha . . . ha . . .

Conductor. [*Pulling out his watch.*] I too have my duties. I'm a state employee.

Professor. [*Turning a little bit to everyone, grotesque and pitiful.*] If you're not interested in my book, you'll be interested to know that I have found a road . . . a road that leads out of the forest . . . I would have freed you all . . . Help me!

Vinedresser. [*To the* Conductor.] Give him a couple of minutes more. Maybe he wants to reconcile himself with God, to seek forgiveness.

Professor. [*With a hysterical voice.*] What do you mean reconciliation and forgiveness! Do you think I asked to come into the world? Do you think I asked to be put together in this stupid way, with the same needs as beasts but with a brain that can conceive of the fourth dimension? [*Turning a little to everyone, like a person hoping to find solidarity.*] Why should I go away now? Why? [*No one answers him.*] Oh, yeah, I get it . . . nothing matters to those who are just watching. You found your tickets, and you're all set for another year. [*With grotesque anger.*] But you aren't! Because the conductor may show up at any minute . . . Every day you hear the train whistling . . . every day. [*To Max.*] And you, too, you who're so cocky . . . Oh, I know . . . I'm familiar with the philosophy of the most recent fools . . . the transcendental "ego," or else the "Stimmung" . . . [*Flying into a rage.*] But what the hell am I saying . . . how can I still talk about these things? . . . [*Screaming.*] We know nothing, neither about ourselves, or about other people, or about the universe! [*Desperately.*] Nothing! Nothing! Nothing! [*Covering his face with his hands.*] But I can't go away just like that, it can't be that we must disappear without having understood . . .

Max. [*Laughing ironically.*] The philosopher's punishment. To disappear without having understood.

Margot. [*Going up to the* Professor *and taking one of his hands.*] I beg you, forget everything you know, everything you've seen, everything you've sought in books. [*The* Professor, *with a sudden impulse, clings to* Margot *terrified, like a baby to his mother, and slowly sinks to the ground, while the woman bends over to support him.*] I'm uneducated, but I've comforted young boys who were dying by merely holding their hand tight in mine . . . like this.

Professor. [*Gasping.*] Yes, yes . . . touch me, hold me, I'm cold, I'm so cold . . . [*To the others.*] I'm trembling, but not with fear . . . no! It's cold, it's just cold.

Margot. [*Caressing his forehead lightly.*] Those young boys forgot that they'd cursed and that they'd killed . . . they forgot that they'd been in my bed . . . they became children again . . . That's it, you have to stretch out, fall asleep.

Professor. [*As if babbling to himself.*] You're right, dear, you're right, but just now I'm following another train of thought . . . faith in bad faith . . . where did I read something like that?

Max. What a hardheaded old bugger! [*To the* Professor.] In a book by one of the most recent and illustrious fools . . . Do you want me to quote the passage?

Professor. No . . . I don't want any quotations!

Vinedresser. [*Coming forward.*] Do you want me to give you absolution? I can do it.

Professor. [*Angrily.*] I don't need absolutions either! [*Drawing close to* Margot *and kissing her hands.*] Tell me . . . tell me again . . . Mama! Daughter! [*The* Vinedresser *kneels down and begins to pray softly.*]

Margot. [*Squatting down and lifting the* Professor's *head, which she props up on her knees.*] That's it, just like that . . . the ground's good, you know? In no other place do you rest so well as on the ground . . . Do you want me to sing you a song from my hometown?

Professor. [*Halfheartedly.*] Night . . . I see night falling, and I know there will be no dawn. [*While music played by stringed instruments softly pervades the air, the woman hums the melody of a kind of lullaby. The other characters, motionless, stare at the dying man, whose suffering gently ceases. Suddenly, the woman stops singing, looks at the Professor, delicately places his head on the grass, lightly touches his eyelids with her fingers, and gets up. The music dies out.*]

Max. [*Lighting his pipe.*] All over? [*With a glance at the dead man while he smokes in small puffs.*] Our teachers weren't worth an iota more than we were . . . [*To the* Vinedresser, *who has remained enraptured with his eyes toward the sky.*] They, too, were bluffing.

Margot. [*Wearily.*] Will you shut up once and for all?

Conductor. [*Touching two fingers to his visor.*] Good evening, everyone! [*He goes off slowly and disappears toward the back of the forest.*]

Max. [*Looking at the dead man.*] I'm sorry on account of my tent . . . He'd promised to mend it . . . Never mind! [*He picks up the tent and covers the corpse with it.*] It will serve as a shroud! [*Silence. Everyone remains motionless.*]

ACT 2

SCENE 1

The theater is dark. The slow opening of the curtain is preceded by blues music heightened occasionally by several voices harmonizing an accompaniment in countersong. The scrim appears, with the seventeenth-century forest in negative, illuminated from behind by an opalescent reflection. The effect should be that of a large X-ray.

The music fades away; some far-off voices are still heard as they gradually disperse; then the scrim is raised, and the forest of debris becomes visible in the rosy light of a sunset. The camping tent has been replaced by a small hut made of rusty corrugated sheet metal. Near the hut there is a strange machine resting on a low pedestal. It is evident that it has been built with odds and ends: coils functioning as pulleys, pieces of twine replacing drive belts, old brush handles for connecting rods, cardboard cogwheels, and so forth. The machine, no wider than a yard and approximately one-and-a-half yards high, must be light and have its parts painted in different colors. Moving any one of the wheels with one's finger will be enough to set the contraption in motion and keep it going for a few minutes, during which time it will give off a soft tinkling sound. Margot, almost at the footlights, with her back to the audience, is looking at the Boy, *who is standing motionless upstage.*

Margot. [*Motioning and in a restrained voice.*] Come on. [*The* Boy *comes forward a few steps, and* Margot *goes toward him but immediately stops because he has retraced his steps.*] No, no . . . I won't move. [*The* Boy *comes forward again and stops a few yards from the woman.* Margot *speaks in a soft, low voice.*] I've been waiting for you for days and nights.

Boy. [*Speaking as if daydreaming.*] Days and nights . . . nights that are black and white . . .

Margot. [*Smiling.*] Black and white, yes . . . or sunset-colored like this evening. I'm alone. They wanted to take me hunting with them, but I refused.

Boy. [*Like an echo.*] Hunting?

Margot. [*In a somewhat familiar tone as if to gain the* Boy's *trust.*] For moles . . . Yes . . . Max says there's nothing but moles and mosquitoes in the forest. The moles live on mosquitoes, and the mosquitoes suck the blood of the moles. A complete ecological cycle, he says . . . [*Becoming aware of the other character's bewilderment.*] Don't try to understand . . . [*Smiling amiably.*] If you were to understand these things, you'd be as unhappy as the others. [*Pause.*] Why don't you come closer?

Boy. [*Moving a few steps closer.*] You've been waiting for me? [*Smiling.*] I, too, knew that one day I'd come looking for you . . . I don't know why.

Margot. On the other hand, I know why I've been waiting for you. I needed to get to know you.

Boy. [*Suddenly not paying attention, pointing to the sheet-metal hut.*] The tent's gone.

Margot. It's under the ground, and then Max replaced it with some sheets of steel that Jack found heaven knows where.

Boy. [*Setting the machine in motion.*] Did the General make this?

Margot. Yes, and he insisted on making a present of it to Max.

Boy. He gives his useless machines to everyone . . . They're very pretty . . . What's this one called?

Margot. Sunflower Thirty-five.

Boy. The one he gave me is called Dancer Alpha. [*Laughing.*] It's got four levers that go up and down alternately [*he imitates with his arms and legs*] as though it were dancing.

Margot. The professor had one that walked. A kind of mechanical spider.

Boy. [*Pensive.*] Maybe we're all useless machines.

Margot. That's not true. You're a poet . . . Jack told me so.

Boy. [*Becoming upset.*] At home they said that to make fun of me. [*As he draws away from the machine.*] Poet . . . [*Flying into a rage.*] It's not true! I've never written a verse.

Margot. There's nothing wrong with being a poet, and you can be one without ever having written a single line. Maybe at home they meant that you were a dreamer, that you had a sensitive disposition.

Boy. I don't know . . .

Margot. But would you like to write poems?

Boy. I have so many things in mind I'm going to write someday.

Margot. Someday, when?

Boy. Someday in my life.

Margot. [*With a somewhat sad smile.*] That's really beautiful . . . to know someday that poetry will come calling. You're young . . . it's a date that's already made for you.

Boy. And yet, I can't wait to grow old.

Margot. Why?

Boy. So I can be right . . . Old people are always right, I'm always wrong.

Margot. Don't be envious of old people's judgment . . . Instead, tell me one of your poems, or what you dream they're going to be like.

Boy. [*Gazing into thin air.*] Once it was in a café. [*Pause.*] In a small café with very few customers, who every evening listened to the same records played on an old phonograph. [*Pause.*] Among these records there was one that was played over and over . . . a sad song, I believe it was from many years back . . . And I was in the café, along with the other people and the phonograph. [*Pause.*] And one evening I saw the singer who had been dead for a long time . . . the singer who had made that record . . . She was sitting at a small table with her chin resting in her hand and was listening. [*Pause.*] The others didn't see her.

Margot. Very nice.

Boy. What?

Margot. The story of this poem you're going to write.

Boy. [*Encouraged.*] I could tell you some others . . . for example, the one about a man who lives alone in a very large city. Alone, I mean, without relatives or friends or anyone, see?

Margot. Yes.

Boy. And so this man wants to die because he's fed up with living alone . . . he wants to throw himself out the window . . . But that very day, a letter comes for him. [*Pause, then smiling as though the story amazes him as well.*] Yeah . . . a letter comes for him, specifically addressed to him, from a woman.

Margot. A woman?

Boy. Yes, the address was written in a woman's handwriting. [*Pause.*] And so the man opens the envelope . . . and there's nothing inside.

Margot. The envelope was empty?

Boy. Yes, empty.

Margot. A joke . . . or else the woman had forgotten to put the letter in the envelope.

Boy. I don't know . . . but the man puts that envelope in his pocket, on the side where his heart is, and decides not to die until he's found the woman who sent the letter . . . And he looks for her, he looks for her through all the streets of the city, for days, for months, for years . . .

Margot. Without finding her?

Boy. Without finding her . . . But in the meantime he's alive. [*Pause.*] And maybe that's why the woman had not put a letter in the envelope.

Margot. Extraordinary! [*Pause.*] And do you think a woman can perform a miracle and save a lonely man, a man who doesn't have anyone and may even want to die?

Boy. In poetry, yes.

Margot. Thank you.

Boy. Why?

Margot. Every time destiny gives me a sign, points out a street to me, makes me understand in a strange way that what I had in mind to do was right, I give thanks. [*With a sad smile.*] I give thanks to . . . to I don't know who. I close my eyes and whisper: Thank you!

Boy. [*Smiling.*] I like to hear you talk. And to look at you, too . . . You're beautiful!

Margot. Beauty's not important.

Boy. Why not?

Margot. It just isn't . . . The years pass by quickly, and I'll grow old.
Boy. What nonsense!
Margot. [*With a sigh.*] It's not nonsense, but never mind. If I could succeed in doing what I have in mind . . .
Boy. [*Sitting down on a small chest.*] Tell me.
Margot. [*Sitting down next to the* Boy.] Helping you go away.
Boy. [*Laughing.*] It's impossible. Nobody's ever left here.
Margot. Don't listen to what the others say. They're all lost souls . . . people without hopes, without feelings . . . Max, for instance, if he wanted to get out of the forest, he could do it.
Boy. How?
Margot. [*Knocking on the little chest with one hand.*] There's a rubber boat in here, with oars, compass, and everything . . . Folded up, it's no bigger than a suitcase. All you have to do is carry it to the bank of the river . . . it's very light.
Boy. And why hasn't he done it?
Margot. Max is a traveler. It's hard to understand what he's thinking . . . you never know when he's coming or going. But don't you tell anyone what I've told you. They'd kill him to get possession of the boat.
Boy. Who would kill him?
Margot. The others . . . the ones who can't go away and who keep receding into time . . . swallowed up by the forest.
Boy. But the two of you will go away, won't you? You'll go up the river in the boat . . . You'll see the world reappear, behind the big trees . . .
Margot. [*Silently laughing while she rests her head on the* Boy's *shoulder.*] If that was the case, I wouldn't have told you the secret. [*Turning slowly around to look into the* Boy's *eyes.*] Haven't you guessed? [*Pause.*] You'll be the one to go away.
Boy. [*Amazed.*] Me?
Margot. [*Embracing him chastely.*] You'll go back to the world. You'll see dawns and sunsets among the living . . . you'll hear clear voices . . . walk over flowery banks, even over sharp rocks, it doesn't matter . . . You'll enjoy the simple pleasures . . . drinking spring water, biting into a fruit . . .
Boy. [*Getting up.*] Don't say any more.
Margot. [*Also getting up.*] Tonight I'll steal the key to the chest, I'll take the boat, and I'll meet you on the riverbank.
Boy. [*Staring into thin air.*] I told you I don't want to hear any more.
Margot. Why?
Boy. We've told some beautiful stories. Let's leave it at that.
Margot. [*Stupefied.*] I don't get it. You don't think what I've been telling you are just fairy tales, do you?

Boy. [*Somewhat annoyed.*] Do you think if it had been a matter of true stories, of real plans for escape, I'd have listened to you? I don't like true stories.

Margot. [*Overcome by a growing excitement.*] What's all this nonsense? You're young, you've got so much life ahead of you . . . obstacles maybe, but it'll be a joy to overcome them.

Boy. No, no joy at all in what you're telling me, in what you'd like to do with me. [*With polite irony.*] To force me to go back to that crowd running through the streets, sweating, telephoning lies with disgust clogging their throats?

Margot. [*Almost stammering.*] But it won't be like that . . . And you were happy listening to me . . . Were you just pretending? And not only just now . . . even when you were telling me about your attempts to get on a ship, to go far away . . .

Boy. [*With calm stubbornness.*] I wasn't pretending at all . . . I was listening to one of my stories, which are sometimes touching, sometimes dramatic. It doesn't matter whether I was telling it to myself or whether you were telling it to me. That's the secret of the dead . . . Haven't you ever seen them smiling serenely with their hands crossed on their chests? Around them people are crying, despairing, asking for forgiveness . . . And they remain serene, smiling, certain they'll no longer have to participate, stretched out wearing handsome new clothes and a gentle smile on their lips. That's why we say they've stopped suffering. I want to stop suffering, too, and that's why I tell myself stories about being dead. Someday the story will come true.

Margot. [*Flying into a rage.*] That's monstrous! Have they hurt you so deeply as all that? But I'll save you in spite of yourself, I'll snatch you away from your damned ghosts, from this false death of yours that's worse than any suicide. [*Becoming elated.*] I'll force you to suffer, yes, to suffer . . . it can be a victory . . . you've never understood it.

Boy. [*With cold politeness.*] For you maybe it'll be a victory . . . not for someone who's already looking forward to his happy disappearance. [*Moving slowly toward the back of the forest.*] Good-bye, Margot.

Margot. [*Screaming.*] No! Stop! [*The* Boy *does not even turn around;* Margot *remains motionless, murmuring halfheartedly.*] The spider web, and all of us are caught up in it. [*Silence, then a swelling of music that is suddenly interrupted. From the left,* Max, Jack, *and the* General *enter making small talk. The latter is stout of build, slightly bald, with a clean-shaven face. He is wearing a well-tailored gray suit, a silk shirt open in front, and felt slippers.* Jack *has the jackboots in his hand.*]

General. [*As though continuing a speech.*] And why did you call it the queen mole?

Jack. [*Conscientiously beginning to brush the boots.*] Because she's as big as a rabbit . . .

General. [*Going toward the machine and thus discovering* Margot, *who has remained motionless as though daydreaming.*] Good day, my beauty. [*Bending over to start the machine.*] How's Sunflower Thirty-five behaving? Does it still respond to your touch? [Margot *does not answer, still staring toward the back of the forest.*]

Max. [*Going into the sheet-metal hut.*] Hi, Margot, what are you brooding about? [*He comes out of the hut with a small battery-operated radio.*] Do you know we discovered the burrow of the queen mole? This time she won't get away from us. [Margot *does not answer. Max, sitting down on a folding stool, starts fiddling around with the small radio as though taking it apart.*]

Jack. [*To* Margot.] The general doesn't believe moles are intelligent.

Max. Our queen mole is quite intelligent; indeed, so much so that she eats the bait without making the trap go off.

General. And what'll you do once you've caught it?

Jack. Here's where we disagree. I'd like to use her coat to clean these boots, which need a good, soft velvet. Mr. Max, however, would like to stuff her.

General. [*Moving away from his machine a short distance and observing its movement with satisfaction.*] Couldn't you tame it? [*He goes back to the machine, draws a small oil can from his pocket, and diligently lubricates some of the hinges.*]

Max. The traps are made with slipknots. You can't tame a dead mole. [*To* Margot.] What do you say about it, Margot?

Margot. [*Squatting down near the machine.*] Do you need my opinion to hang moles?

Max. But I'll need your help to stuff her.

General. [*To* Max.] You know how to stuff moles?

Max. I should say so! Taxidermy is one of my hobbies.

Jack. Tax . . . ?

Max. Taxidermy . . . the art of preparing and preserving animal skins in lifelike poses.

General. And what's the pose of your queen mole?

Max. Oh, a thousand poses, from flirtatious to scornful, from peaceful to aggressive, from deceptive to innocent . . . She's not a female for nothing. [*To* Margot.] Margot! Wake up. Don't you feel like talking?

Margot. [*Wearily.*] I'm fascinated by Sunflower Thirty-five.

General. Good for you! That's precisely why useless machines are so useful . . . They fascinate whoever looks at them, they give a rhythm to thoughts and slowly neutralize them . . .

Margot. [*As though to herself.*] Our elders watched the flames in the fireplace.

General. [*Evidently satisfied with her observation.*] Precisely . . . but nowadays there are no more fireplaces . . . hence my machines. I once built one that was hypnotic, with little shiny balls that ran after each other in concentric circles. Staring at it for just five minutes was enough to put you to sleep . . . I also had it patented.

Margot. And did you have beautiful dreams?

General. [*Somewhat mortified.*] I haven't gotten that far yet. But you could try . . . Not, of course, with machines like these, built with odds and ends . . .

Max. [*Laughing ironically.*] Cybernetics . . . mankind's last hope. After they've done our thinking for us, someday machines will do our suffering for us. [*Angrily shaking the small radio.*] This one, however, doesn't want to work. [*Putting it close to his ear.*] And yet it's making a sputtering sound. [*Turning the dials.*] Let's see whether it plays . . . [*Pause.*] What the hell! It sputters, but it doesn't talk. [*To* Margot.] It's just like you. [*Flinging the small radio into the underbrush.*] To hell with it! [*Suddenly an unpleasant, noisy voice is heard.*]

Voice on the Radio. . . . send your application along with twenty-five cents in stamps, enclosing the birth certificate and the marital status of the applicant, to the ministry of . . .

Max. [*He dashes over to retrieve the apparatus.*] Now we're cooking! [*The radio has already become silent.*] Come on, give! [*He shakes it, lays it on the ground, and crouches in front it, looking at it with hostile eyes.*]

Margot. We'll never know which ministry those applications were supposed to be sent to.

Jack. [*Continuing to brush the boots vigorously.*] It would have been better if you'd brought along a radio transmitter.

Max. To send out some SOS's?

Jack. Some curse words, too. [*Taking the boots over to the* General *and standing them up in front of him.*] Here you go, General; they are two mirrors!

General. [*Fitting his monocle into his eye and bending over to examine them.*] Thanks, my boy, they're quite impressive.

Jack. [*With a certain amount of pride.*] When I found them, I had a premonition. I said, this foretells an important meeting . . . two days later you arrived.

General. [*Patiently.*] And from that moment on you've persisted in

offering them to me . . . But I've told you they're too big for me
. . . and besides, I've never worn jackboots.

Jack. [*Taking back the boots and returning to his pump, somewhat disappointed.*] I know, you prefer slippers. What a shame! [*To* Max.]
The one time I find a general who honors me with his friendship . . .

Max. [*Finishing the sentence.*] . . . he doesn't wear either epaulets or
medals, and he goes around in slippers . . . [*Pauses, then changing his tone.*] On the other hand, there's one thing I've never
understood . . . a man who hates bosses and adores generals . . .

Jack. [*Smiling, somewhat embarrassed.*] Yes, I've got to admit it, I like
them.

Margot. [*To* Jack, *the way one speaks to a child.*] The General is no
longer in the service.

General. [*Gently stubborn.*] And even when I was in the service, I
never wore jackboots.

Max. Not even when you rode on horseback?

General. [*Calmly.*] I've never ridden a horse . . . As a junior officer
I went around on foot. I fought the first war in the infantry.
Then I joined the general staff. Twenty years behind a desk
carefully preparing mobilization plans that, in practice, had to
be done over from beginning to end. Finally, I fought the last
war in an automobile.

Margot. On the battlefield in an automobile?

General. No, I was far removed from the battlefield. The battlefield was on the table in front of me. Some tiny flags wrapped
around pins, aerial reconnaissance photographs, signal corps
reports, telephone, radio . . .

Max. And from that desk you commanded the action?

General. Not at all . . . I only gave my opinion on the use of the
tank forces. I'm an expert on the subject. All my life I've worked
with nothing but tanks, from their construction to their tactical
use . . . Good points and bad points, history and traditions,
psychology and aggressive spirit of the armored division troops.

Margot. How many millions of men do you think you've had
massacred during your career?

General. I don't know . . . I've never concerned myself with statistics.

Max. And what effect did it have on you? [*Correcting himself.*] Oh,
yeah, you never saw the dead. You stayed behind that desk of
yours.

General. [*Gravely.*] Yes, in fact, I couldn't even see my own dead.

Margot. Your what?

General. [*Going back over to the machine, which has stopped, and setting it back in motion.*] I had a family, too, you know. [*As if speaking to himself.*] One day I received a message. "You are kindly requested to present yourself at Area Headquarters for communications that concern you." The message was marked confidential and urgent . . . At Area Headquarters I find solemn faces, I hear rounds of little coughs, and I'm bombarded with pats on the shoulder. The Area commander, a character who's anything but friendly, starts calling me by my first name . . . I wanted to scream out: I get it! Tell me quickly whether it's my wife or my children, and who's dead and who's been wounded . . . Nothing. [*Touching his throat.*] I couldn't pronounce a word . . . a kind of paralysis here . . . And all around me more rounds of coughing. Then they start talking about an air raid, as though everybody knew about it . . . and finally they shove me into another automobile . . . "You'll receive further information at army headquarters" . . . [*Pause, then with an ambiguous gesture.*] And so on . . . from headquarters to headquarters . . .

Margot. Dead?

General. All of them . . . my wife and the three children. A seventeen-year-old girl, two boys, one fifteen and the other twelve . . . [*Wiping his face with one of his hands.*] How did we end up talking about my family? [*To Max.*] Ah, it was you . . . you said I never saw the dead. Yes, but I would like at least to have seen my own. I felt like I had the right. But I didn't. The whole thing was absurd, something about the complete destruction of an entire district of the city . . . [*Slight pause.*] It was in the summer, they had had to dig some large mass graves in a hurry, putting in a lot of lime and a lot of phenol . . . [*Pause.*] Then I got the notion of identifying at least the house . . . I wandered around for three days over mountains of ruins . . . I'd have settled for a small shoe, hell, for a coffeepot. [*He laughs quietly.*] But where was the house? Where was the street? Where were the trees along the avenue? [*As if to himself.*] Because there should have been an avenue there . . . an avenue where, coming home from school, my kids . . . [*He breaks off, remaining petrified, with his face convulsed, then resumes with detached calm.*] After three days I was back in front of my table . . . with the topographical map, the little flags, the telephone . . .

Max. And you didn't ask yourself who was responsible?

General. [*In a toneless voice.*] Sure, I asked myself that. [*Pause.*] It could be the Germans or the Americans, the petty politicians or the bankers . . . [*Pause.*] And if it had been me? If I'd been the one responsible? [*Pause.*] From this question there arose others. I began to ask myself: Why are you living? What's the sense of everything you've done? Because, if I'm the one responsible, that means I've blundered everything, from the very beginning, from the first day of my life . . . [*Pause, then with his customary terrible, quiet laugh.*] I was afraid of going mad . . . I saw myself in a strait jacket, with the hospital orderlies holding me by the wrists . . . I became afraid, terribly afraid. Then I tried to take refuge in my memories, but I quickly realized that the bombs had destroyed the past as well. [*Beginning to move toward the left and making gestures.*] For instance . . . what was my daughter's voice like when she used to say . . . [*Standing still and raising his voice.*] But what did my daughter used to say? And why would she laugh? But then was she really laughing? [*Shouting as he goes off left.*] Well then, what was my baby's mouth like, what were her eyes like, what was her hair like? [*His voice fades offstage in a kind of sob.* Jack *and* Max *have followed the* General's *exit with their eyes and thus are unaware that the* Vinedresser *has appeared behind them.* Margot, *however, has seen him.*]

Vinedresser. Good evening. [Max *does not answer.* Jack *remains lost in thought.* Margot *continues somewhat uneasily watching the newcomer, as though she senses or fears something.*]

Max. [*Turning slowly around toward the* Vinedresser.] Do you want me to go?

Vinedresser. That's not necessary.

Margot. [*To* Max.] Why do you want to go?

Max. Just a feeling I've got . . . You know I'm subject to forebodings, to premonitions. [*To the* Vinedresser, *laughing ironically.*] A kind of seismographer.

Margot. What kind of forebodings?

Max. Nothing definite. [*Nodding toward the* Vinedresser.] As soon as he appeared, there was something like a moment of suspension, and I felt it wasn't for me.

Vinedresser. [*Somewhat embarrassed.*] I assure you that . . .

Max. Don't assure me of anything. You don't know how to lie . . . [*To* Margot, *with a hint of sadness.*] You'll be the one who'll lie, afterward . . .

Margot. [*Flying into a rage.*] What lies have I told you?

Max. Who knows? I never thought about cataloging them. Or even of exposing them. I'm too lazy. [*To the* Vinedresser.] And anyway, the boundaries are always so vague between a lie and a truth . . . [*With sudden resolution.*] Besides, I'm dying to go see whether the queen mole has fallen into the trap. [*Smiling.*]

Recently, my interests have been centered on the lives of moles
. . . A little animal that hasn't yet been studied as much as it
deserves. Maybe someday a book will come out on it.

Margot. [*To the* Vinedresser.] Don't believe him, he's not going
after moles.

Max. Well, after what, then? Elephants? That'd be more picturesque, but there aren't any. [*To* Jack.] Have you ever seen any
elephants around here?

Jack. No, sir.

Margot. You're going away because you're afraid.

Max. Of you?

Margot. Of what I'm capable of saying. You've always been a
coward. You play like you're such a superman, you don't admit
that you can be surprised by events . . . but I'll fix you. I'll tell
you now . . . I'm leaving!

Max. [*Calmly.*] Who with?

Margot. By myself.

Max. [*To the* Vinedresser, *smiling.*] First lie. She's never gone away
alone . . . When she comes back, that's when she's alone. When
the men have gotten tired of her and have driven her away like
a bitch, that's when she comes back alone and whimpering.

Margot. When did you ever see me come back whimpering?
When? You were the one who'd come running after me. [*To the*
Vinedresser, *in a spiteful, mocking tone.*] You can't imagine how
he begs for mercy, the sentimental scenes that he makes.

Max. [*In an annoyed tone.*] Oh, of course he can picture it. Who
knows how many men and women he's seen despising each
other and yet neither able to get along without the other . . . Do
you actually think a doctor of souls would be shocked by so
little?

Margot. [*To the* Vinedresser.] And when he wants to kill himself?
But he's never gone through with it! His kind don't kill themselves.

Max. That's right . . . men like me live, which is much harder. [*To*
Jack.] Shall we go?

Jack. Right away, sir. [*The two of them move off.* Max *whistles the tune
we heard* Jack *play on his harmonica.* Margot *and the* Vinedresser
have remained motionless.]

Margot. [*Suddenly turning around.*] Well, then? What is it?

Vinedresser. [*Somewhat embarrassed.*] It's nothing . . . first of all you
have to promise me you'll keep calm, Margot.

Margot. [*Suspicious.*] How come you've decided to start calling me
by my first name?

Vinedresser. The way I would a daughter . . .

Margot. [*As if to herself.*] It's a strange time of day for you to come here . . . Max leaves . . . [*Giving a start.*] Did he put you up to preaching to me?

Vinedresser. Nobody put me up to it. And anyway, preaching to you . . .

Margot. A waste of breath, isn't it? I'm not redeemable . . . [*Pause.*] When I was in the sanatorium . . . [*Laughing.*] Don't worry, I went there because I was the mistress of one of the doctors . . . In the sanatorium, as I was saying, there were cases marked "negative with a double cross" . . . do you know what that means in hospital jargon? The hopeless.

Vinedresser. [*With a sigh.*] Well then?

Margot. Nothing . . . Consider me a negative with a double cross . . . Give me the last rites if you really care about it, and let me ruin myself.

Vinedresser. I give the last rites only to those who are dying . . . as I did a few moments ago.

Margot. [*Giving a start.*] What does that mean?

Vinedresser. [*Bowing his head.*] The Boy . . .

Margot. [*With a cry.*] Is he sick? What's wrong?! Speak up.

Vinedresser. [*In a hollow voice.*] He is dead.

Margot. [*Painfully.*] Dead? It's not true! You're lying! [*Rushing toward the* Vinedresser *and shaking him.*] Why are you so spiteful? What have I ever done to you? Speak up!

Vinedresser. I asked you to keep calm.

Margot. [*Screaming.*] But what's happened? Why dead? Who killed him?

Vinedresser. No one. He wanted to die.

Margot. [*Drawing back with her eyes wide open.*] It's not possible . . . Did he kill himself?

Vinedresser. Not exactly . . . in any case, I gave him the last rites . . . He let himself die . . . You know perfectly well he lived in a world of his own. I'd gone looking for him, as I often did, in the hut made out of branches down by the river. He was stretched out on his pallet, and he told me his death . . .

Margot. He told you . . .

Vinedresser. Yes. I thought he was talking nonsense, like he usually did, like when he'd talk with his mother and with his sister . . . [*Pause.*] Then I understood that it was the truth . . . By telling his death he was making it come true . . . at a certain point he asked me for the last rites. I told him there were certain things you don't joke about, and he answered me that he wasn't joking. When he dozed off . . . [*He covers his face with his hands and is too upset to continue.*]

Margot. But how is that possible? And you didn't do anything? Didn't you try to get help? [*Raving.*] No, I can't believe it, you're hiding the truth from me, you don't want to admit his suicide . . . Oh, now I get it . . . you'd deny the evidence of the sun, if the sun put one of your dogmas in doubt.

Vinedresser. There was nothing to do . . . I asked him if he'd taken any poison . . . He didn't have any wounds . . . He answered me with a smile: "I've drunk life down to the last drop . . ." Then he closed his eyes, and slowly . . . the way you fall asleep . . .

Margot. But why?! Why?! [*Raising her arms.*] Oh my God, my God, help me! [*Overwhelmed with growing desperation.*] I didn't know how to save him! [*Raving.*] I talked to him about leaving, about rescues, about resurrections . . . [*With an outbreak of shrill laughter.*] You stupid woman! Stupid! You wanted poetry, feelings . . . you wanted to play at being an honest woman . . .

Vinedresser. [*Frightened.*] What are you babbling about? . . . Try to be reasonable.

Margot. [*Overwhelmed with growing excitement.*] Ah, me babbling? Oh, sure . . . you can't understand . . . that's why you're in the forest. [*Screaming.*] You don't realize I was supposed to stick to my part, to the role that was assigned to me! I was supposed to remain a whore! A whore! And I would have saved him . . . [*Speeding up her words.*] I was afraid he'd think it was a whim of mine . . . But no, not even that . . . I followed a vain, foolish impulse . . . the sinful woman redeeming herself in the pure eyes of the innocent . . . and instead I should have undressed at once . . . fought with the only weapon I've got . . . My flesh! My flesh!

Vinedresser. [*Energetically.*] Don't blaspheme!

Margot. [*More and more painfully.*] Oh, yeah . . . for you truth is blasphemy! [*Flying into a rage.*] But what if woman's destiny is this? . . . The same destiny as the earth's . . . the hoe, earthquakes, mud, spit! [*Spreading her arms in a kind of exaltation.*] Men can't understand that there's joy even in being beaten, insulted, degraded. The earth! You are plows, spades, manure . . . You are violence, pride, knowledge! But it is earth, on the other hand, that allows itself to be trampled . . . The earth, which is eternal, boundless, always the same and always different . . . And you, ever so tiny. [*Bursting into laughter.*] How comical you are with all your knowledge! Max not believing, and you believing . . . Each one convinced he has a monopoly on infallible truths . . . Knowledge, God . . . And me in the middle, ignorant, pitiful, defenseless . . . but the darkness is the same for all, the darkness of the forest . . . only a small light far off . . . No, damn it all! There is no light! [*Practically tearing her jacket off her back.*] Do you see this? Future food for worms. Future dust, earth . . . this flesh of mine, I was supposed to offer it to him . . . [*With sudden resolution.*] I want to go where he is . . . I want him to see me as I am . . . as I ought to have been . . . [*Running toward the back of the forest.*] Here I am . . . here I am . . . naked! naked! . . . [Margot's *cries fade off in the back. It is almost completely dark onstage. The* Vinedresser *has fallen on his knees and has his hands joined together. The curtain slowly closes, and the eerie projection of the forest appears on the scrim.*]

SCENE 2

Night has passed, and dawn is about to break. It is announced by a rustling symphony for strings, while the forest brightens into a milky halo from which the debris gradually emerges, as is the case with images on photographic film that has been immersed in the developing bath. Onstage there is only the General, *who is smoking a cigarette and standing motionless near his useless machine. After a few moments, the voice of* Jack *is heard in the distance.*

Jack. General . . . General! [*The* General *does not answer, nor does he turn around.* Jack *comes forth into the clearing in the foreground.*] No one . . . [*As he heads toward the gasoline pump, he mutters.*] Very likely he, too, has gone wading around in the river in his slippers. [*Glancing at the jackboots.*] He could have at least put them on this time . . . [*Suddenly turning around.*] Huh? [*Pause.*] Who spoke? [*Taking cover behind the pump.*] Let's not kid around. [*He peers toward the hut as he bends down to pick up a massive monkey wrench that he brandishes menacingly.*] Who's there? [*Standing still and continuing to smoke, the* General *watches* Jack. Jack *pants.*] No one.
General. [*In a calm and somewhat annoyed voice.*] Will you wake up?
Jack. [*Jumping.*] Who's there? [*He takes a couple of steps.*] Oh . . . it's you . . .
General. [*With a sigh.*] At last!
Jack. [*Somewhat confused.*] I wasn't sleeping . . .
General. [*Dropping his cigarette butt and crushing it with his foot.*] Worse . . . You were going around within yourself . . . you were going around in the maze of your own sickness, to the point of not seeing me. [*Pause.*] And what do you plan to do with that thing?
Jack. [*Throwing down the tool.*] Excuse me . . . I thought I saw . . .

General. Ghosts.

Jack. One . . . just one.

General. Who?

Jack. I don't know who he is. He hangs around the gasoline pump with his head split open like a watermelon and looks at me with that eye that stayed open that night.

General. And were you alone that night as well?

Jack. [*Lowering his head.*] Yes.

General. And a man was passing by.

Jack. He was whistling a tune . . . I wanted to warn him, to shout out for him to run away . . . I felt my hands searching for the hammer, taking hold of it . . . [*Putting his hands to his face, he sobs.*] Oh . . .

General. [*Drawing close to* Jack.] Don't think about it. [*Giving him a couple of pats on the back.*] Let's have a smoke on it. [*He offers him a cigarette.*]

Jack. [*Taking the cigarette.*] Thanks. [*Pause.*] I wanted to explain to you . . .

General. For God's sake, don't start up again. All we do is take turns worrying each other with our self-justifications. My fault, your fault, the other guy's fault . . . [*To himself.*] We're grotesque.

Jack. Excuse me . . . It's been years since I've spoken with anyone, years that I have stifled inside myself . . . [*He breaks off, touching his chest with his benumbed hands.*]

General. [*Pacing his words slowly.*] I know, but I wouldn't be able to help you in any way . . . all of us are impotent when confronted with executions . . . [*Pause.*] Once during the war . . . I mean the other war, when I was a junior officer, I had to witness an execution by firing squad. I was under orders. A kind of rotating duty that fell to us every now and then. Maybe the commanding general thought he was providing us with some diversion. Anyhow, it was the first time I saw a man shot . . . it's very different from what you think it's like . . . It was a question of a sergeant who had deserted because his wife was cheating on him . . . a Southerner . . . When he found himself in front of the firing squad, he stood at attention and, turning to the highest ranking officer present, he said: "General, I assure you that, if they'd given me the time to do it, I'd have killed my wife and then come back to perform my duties in the trenches. I'm not a coward . . ." The general answered: "I know, my boy, but there is nothing I can do about it. I have to follow orders just like you . . ." The sergeant said: "I understand, general . . ." and that was all.

Jack. Did he die at once?

General. No. At the first volley he fell forward, then lifted up his head and turned to look at us as if to say: "Hey, what's going on?" Then the squad commander gave the order to fire again. [*In the transparent haze is heard the chirping of a couple of birds.*]

Jack. [*Looking upward, he attempts a timid warble, then mutters.*] They don't believe in it any more . . . [*Observing the* General, *who darts his eyes about.*] Now *you*'re seeing things . . .

General. [*Continuing to move his head here and there.*] Flies . . . Recently I've been studying the flight of flies, and I think I have a rather interesting hunch. The fly is capable of perceiving every deviation from its course because the vibrations of its wings have a gyroscopic function that the man-made helicopter, for instance, lacks.

Jack. [*Hunching his shoulders.*] Machines . . . always machines, you don't think about anything but machines.

General. That's true, it's one of my weaknesses. On the other hand, machines are optimistic. They're the most tangible expression of power and happiness. They give a sense of well-being, of confidence, as does everything that is the result of a mathematical calculation. Trains, steamships, electric turbines, they're all toys for adults, and they console man for his imperfection.

Jack. Surely there must have been a time when men lived without machines.

General. Yes, after the chaos . . . When men and beasts were one and the same and ate each other by turns, and they slept in caves or in trees. But one day, a living being very much like all the other monkeys managed, with some sharp rocks, to slice the trunk of a tree . . . The wheel was born, and with that the monkey had become a man.

Jack. The Vinedresser says God was the one who made men different from beasts.

General. Could be, but the first sign of that difference was without a doubt the wheel. And from that day on, man has not been able to do without machines . . . he has kept on making increasingly perfect ones, including the helicopter that I was thinking about a minute ago.

Jack. [*Laughing ironically.*] Now a helicopter that'd come pick us up wouldn't be such a bad idea.

General. So we could go where?

Jack. [*Somewhat embarrassed.*] Ah, that's another story!

General. See . . . all of you just beat your heads against the windowpane like horseflies.

Jack. [*Nervously.*] That's enough of that . . . flies, horseflies, I'll end up hearing them buzzing around inside my head. [Max *silently appears in the back and comes forward with weary steps.*]

General. [*Without even looking at him.*] Any news?

Max. [*Flinging himself down wearily on one of the small chests.*] No . . . The Vinedresser's keeping up the search.

Jack. The Vinedresser knows the forest like nobody else . . . If she's still around, he'll find her for sure.

Max. [*Flying off the handle.*] If she's still around?! Where could she go? [*With sudden anger.*] Anyway, it doesn't matter to me!

General. On this point, you'd better get things straight with yourself. Does it matter to you whether she comes back, or doesn't it?

Max. [*Wearily.*] I don't know. At any rate, Margot has always come back before.

General. Forgive me if I'm persistent . . . I know I'm being indiscreet . . .

Max. [*With an ironic smile.*] Indiscretion in the forest . . .

General. It's a theory I've held ever since I was a young man . . . Women who walk the streets of a city, of whatever city you want, are always the same . . . And men desire them . . .

Max. Out of curiosity.

General. That's it exactly, curiosity for the novel . . . but novel in what way?

Max. And you think that's all the more reason why a man shouldn't have any curiosity for a woman like Margot, whom I've known since time immemorial. [*As if to himself.*] Maybe ever since I was born . . . [*Pause.*] It's not easy to answer you . . . I could tell you that it's just a trick on the part of nature, or else that we never succeed in completely knowing a human being, whether it's a man or a woman . . . or yet again, that what we assume to be our curiosity is only anxiety and the desire to be judged.

General. To be judged . . . Yes, I believe that's one of man's fundamental needs . . . We fear judgment, but we seek it out.

Max. [*As if speaking to himself.*] And then, every one of Margot's homecomings was astounding. She had a hundred ways of reappearing, and each one of them different. Sometimes they were dramatic, sometimes childlike. She had always lost something and acquired something else.

General. For instance?

Max. Unexpected gestures, flashes that would transform her. [*With sudden weariness.*] Then she'd fall asleep with her hands in her lap, enigmatic and childlike. [*Pause.*] One day I decided to kill her. I quietly cocked the pistol and put the muzzle to her temple . . . In her sleep Margot made a gesture with her hand, like so . . . as though she were chasing away a butterfly. [*Pause.*] I put the pistol back in my pocket. [*A pause during which the quiet laughter of the* General *is heard.*] What are you laughing at?

General. Just because. I think the same thing happens with the impulse to kill as happens with certain diseases. We think we are the only ones who've suffered from it; then . . . [*In a gently grotesque tone.*] Me, too . . . me, too . . . me, too . . . [*He quietly laughs to himself.*]

Max. [*Getting up and looking toward the back of the forest.*] What's keeping the Vinedresser? Do you suppose he's thrown himself in the river, too?

General. [*Good-naturedly.*] Don't be melodramatic. Anyway, the river isn't as dangerous as you think.

Max. You can drown just as easily in calm water. I was thinking about it a moment ago . . .

General. In connection with what?

Max. Something that happened once . . . I was on the shore of a lake, and I noticed some people watching a certain point. A child had disappeared in the water, and the boatmen were looking for the boy, dragging the bottom with poles . . . A crowd gathered. Then the weeping mother arrived, and they gave her a chair. After a while the people began to thin out . . . Some had to go to work, others to fix lunch. Even the boatmen, after a while, gave up their search . . . Only the mother remained, sitting in her chair, screaming. Then she, too, calmed down. Every now and again a relative would go console her . . . At a certain point one of these women said: "I put the potatoes on the kitchen table, five pounds for sixty cents . . ." "Fifty-five . . .", said the mother, correcting her.

General. [*Smiling.*] All of us are little cogwheels, and we can't get out of the gearworks.

Max. The future generations will be nothing but gearworks; they'll go around arm in arm with robots.

General. Then the robots will get the upper hand, stage a coup d'état, and subjugate mankind. The world will be ruled by robots.

Max. [*As if to himself.*] They'll take the place of God; they will recreate and organize a cosmos according to the laws of mathematical calculation. Maybe that's the goal and raison d'être of tomorrow's generations.

Jack. [*To* Max.] Speaking of machines, would you mind letting me
have your little radio? I want to see if I can make it work.

Max. [*Making a vague gesture toward the bushes.*] I don't know where
I threw it.

Jack. I'll look for it. [*He starts wandering around in the bushes, but
when he reaches the area surrounding the gallows, he halts, hesitant
and almost fearful.*]

Max. [*As if to himself.*] In an inlet of the river some rust-colored
roots were cropping up, as fine as hair.

General. [*As if to himself.*] Once, on a holiday in the country, I
helped some farmers assemble their threshing machine. The
opening for the grain was painted red, the grain itself was a
bright yellow. My wife was wearing a summery dress that was
. . . what color was it? I don't know . . . I've never been able to
remember the color of that dress. [*Pause, then to* Jack.] What the
hell are you doing?

Jack. [*Pointing to the bushes at the base of the gallows.*] The radio set is
over there.

General. Then why don't you get it?

Jack. Suppose while I'm bending over, the noose comes down?

General. [*Snorting and somewhat annoyed.*] Oh, my God! [*He goes and
picks up the radio and hands it over to* Jack.] There!

Jack. Thanks. [*He quickly comes away, goes over and squats down next to
the pump and starts taking the small set apart with a screwdriver.*]

Max. [*Still looking toward the back of the forest.*] Let's hope the Vinedresser remembers his appointment.

General. Sure he'll remember it . . . He's a good guy, even if you
don't like him.

Max. [*Shrugging his shoulders.*] Why shouldn't I like him? We travel
different roads, that's all. Some people cling desperately to the
past, while others reach out, with just as much desperation,
toward the future. [*As if to himself.*] What's the use of saving a
civilization that's dead?

General. Do you think it's possible to construct a new one out of it?

Max. Maybe . . . And that's why you consider me a visionary. But
today there is no other choice. You can either give up hope or
become a visionary.

General. Those who give up hope have the consolation of believing
in a reward in the hereafter.

Max. [*Flying into a rage.*] Oh, eternal life! It's enough to drive you
crazy just thinking about it.

Jack. [*Waving the small radio.*] It's working! [*Triumphantly.*] I figured there was something wrong with the batteries. [*To the* General.] The acid had corroded the lead and formed some mold.

General. Some effloresence.

Jack. What? Uh . . . the thing that makes contact difficult . . .

General. So it works now?

Jack. [*Going over to put the small radio on the roof of the hut so it can be readily seen by the audience.*] It'll work as soon as it's daylight and the stations come on the air. [*The* Vinedresser *has appeared at the edge of the forest. He is tired, spattered with mud, and very pale.*]

General. [*With a hint of irony.*] Oh, here's our messenger! Now we'll hear the latest.

Jack. Well?

Vinedresser. I found her!

Max. [*Without even concealing his anxiety.*] You saw Margot? Where is she?

Vinedresser. Roaming around the forest.

Max. Did you speak to her?

Vinedresser. I tried to ask her some questions, but she acted like she didn't see me. She kept looking at me . . . Something must have snapped inside.

Max. [*Impatiently.*] So you don't know if she's coming back?

Vinedresser. Where else can she go?

Max. Will she come back to me?

Vinedresser. I don't know.

Max. [*Stamping his foot angrily on the ground.*] She's always come back to me. Maybe she's lost something and acquired something else . . . I was saying so a minute ago.

Vinedresser. Maybe she's lost everything and found everything. Maybe she no longer needs anyone. Even her silence is an indication . . . Whoever is wrapped in silence is forced to listen to the voice of God.

Max. [*Suspiciously eyeing the* Vinedresser.] Whoever is wrapped in silence . . . [Margot *has appeared among the trees; she stops in the distance and observes the group of men. Her clothing is torn in many places and is spattered with mud. She comes forward, and a great silence falls. She seems calm and softly sings a legion song of which the tune is discernible more than anything else.*]

Margot.

> Moi je ne suis pas d'carton
> et ladiga, ladiga, ladèga . . .
> J'ai bien trop aimé dit-on
> et ladiga, ladèga, ladà.

Max. [*With ill-concealed anxiety.*] Margot . . .

Margot. [*Going over to the machine and starting the wheels gently moving.*]

> Vive les gars de la Légion
> et ladiga, ladiga, ladèga . . .
> Qui s'enivrent à leur façon
> et ladiga, ladèga, ladà . . .

Max. Margot, listen to me.

Vinedresser. [*Gently mediating.*] Let her sing . . . It's a way of freeing herself.

Margot. [*To the* Vinedresser, *with a slight giggle.*] Do you like the songs of legionnaires? They seem like nursery rhymes for children, and the desert wind scatters them. [*She starts singing again.*]

> Si tu rêves à une femme très chic
> et ladiga, ladiga, ladèga . . .
> Il faut avoir pas mal de fric
> et ladiga, ladèga, ladà . . .

Max. [*Looking at the others as though seized by a foreboding.*] What's going on, what is it?

Vinedresser. [*To* Max.] I told you something had snapped.

Margot. [*To the* Vinedresser.] The glaciers bloom in springtime . . . Watch out, Vinedresser . . . [*To* Max.] And who are you? I don't know you . . . You run between two glass walls and you see everything, but not your own soul.

Max. [*Controlling himself.*] Margot, listen to me. We'll go away . . . You know that I came here of my own free will and that I've got the means to go away whenever I want. We'll be the only ones saved.

Jack. [*Laughing softly.*] The only ones saved . . . This I've got to see.

General. [*Good-naturedly, to* Max.] Try to keep at least your own wits about you.

Max. [*To the* General, *flying into a rage.*] Don't interrupt me! *I* know how to talk to Margot. [*To* Margot, *tenderly.*] You've always believed me, haven't you?

Margot. [*Moving from one of them to the next, with the undulating step of someone following the rhythm of a dance that is barely hinted at.*] I've believed everybody. [*To the* Vinedresser.] Even you, poor swordless angel . . .

Max. [*Imperiously.*] Margot, I forbid you . . .

Margot. [*To the* General.] And you, gnawing your tail like a scorpion in the circle of fire. [*To* Jack.] And even you, who are the most pitiful of all, with nothing but a harmonica to lull your despair.

Max. [*Almost imploring.*] Margot . . . You once told me that you have always spent your life asking for pity without wanting it . . . Let me at least this once ask it for myself.

Margot. [*As though dreaming.*] Pity? No one asks for it any more. Everybody's proud, everybody's powerful and very rich. Gone are the days when people asked for pity. Pity is dead. [*In the distance is heard the sound of the tom-tom, and everyone, except* Max *and* Margot, *turns toward the back of the forest and remains listening.*]

Max. [*To Margot.*] Margot . . . Listen to me.

General. [*To* Max, *with sudden harshness.*] Will you cut out that whining? [*The sound of the tom-tom is repeated.*]

Jack. [*Moving a few steps toward the forest.*] The signal . . .

General. [*Starting to go.*] At last!

Max. [*Looking around himself with anguish.*] You can't be leaving?

Jack. [*To* Max, *almost joyfully.*] The signal . . . Didn't you hear? Someone's arrived . . .

General. [*Who has already started off toward the forest.*] Let's go, Jack . . . Let's go meet the new guests.

Max. No! Stop! Don't leave me alone! [*To the* Vinedresser, *who has taken a few steps.*] Stop, Vinedresser . . . I don't want to be left alone!

Vinedresser. [*With a hint of sadness.*] No one is alone, and no one is forsaken . . . There is someone watching over all of us.

Max. [*In despair.*] The silence! [*Stretching out his arms toward the* Vinedresser, *who is moving off.*] The silence, no! Vinedresser . . . [Max *remains panting and motionless with his arms hanging at his sides. The* Vinedresser *has continued on his way and has disappeared into the forest, along with the others, toward the place where the last beats of the tom-tom are resounding.* Max *comes back toward* Margot.] Margot . . . I'm afraid . . . Margot . . . [Margot *does not answer.* Max, *almost stammering.*] Between the two of us there have been days and nights, human relations, habits . . . [*Almost with rage.*] Love, yes! Why should I be ashamed of that word? [*To the woman, with beseeching eyes.*] Isn't that perhaps true? Speak up . . . Please, speak up . . . Do you want me to grovel? Do you want me to admit I've been wrong? Say something for pity's sake . . . Insult me if you want . . . [Margot *silently begins to retreat toward the forest.* Max's *eyes are wide open.*] No! Don't go away! [*Screaming.*] Margot . . . Margot! [*Realizing what she is about to do,*

he lets out a scream of horror and turns toward the audience, covering his face with his hands. Margot *has reached the gallows, has turned around in profile, and calmly looks at the top of it.* Max *gnashes his teeth in terror and dares not turn around.*] No! Don't do it, Margot . . . If you leave me, I'm lost . . . Margot! [*The radio set, on the roof of the sheet-metal hut, suddenly starts broadcasting. At first a gay chiming of bells, then the usual anonymous and somewhat nasal voice.*]
Voice on the Radio. Ladies and gentlemen, good morning. The time is eight o'clock . . . In a few minutes we'll broadcast the news report and the stock quotations. In the meantime we invite you to take part in our fifteenth lesson in rhythmic gymnastics, which will benefit your physical as well as your spiritual well-being. [*Some soft music, precisely that of rhythmical gymnastics, will accompany the voice on the radio.*] Forward arm stretch . . . One . . . and! Backward arm stretch . . . Two . . . and! [Max, *like a marionette, begins frantically performing the exercises.*] Sideways arm stretch . . . One . . . and! Downward arm stretch . . . Two . . . and! [Max, *staring straight ahead with his eyes wide open, his face to the audience, continues performing the movements designated by the radio.*] Touch your toes, keeping your arms and legs straight . . . One . . . and! [*From the top part of the gallows a rope with a noose uncoils lazily, like a snake, and descends far enough to brush against* Margot's *face. The voice on the radio, the music, and the wild gymnastics of* Max *continue as the curtain slowly falls.*]

The End

The Seige

A Play in Two Acts

by
Ezio d'Errico

Translated by Louis Kibler

Characters

Isaac
Ariadne
The Reporter
Chanusky
Tanya
Moko
Chalcedony
Cosmo
Mr. Brandolisio

Act 1

A junk dealer's warehouse as vast as a cathedral and as ingenious as a termite nest rises vertically to the upper floors, which are reached by thin, narrow iron ladders. Open transverse balconies covered with cobwebs complicate the architecture of this beehive of old rags, which, to judge from a large trap door in the floor, continues down into the basement. Among the piles of household furnishings, bundles of paper destined for the pulp mills, and ragged draperies appear tunnels, galleries, secret passages; one can imagine connecting trenches, at whose intersections greenish mirrors in gilded frames disorient customers by casting distorted perspectives. Phonographs with horns, amphorae encrusted with deep-sea shells, brass lamps, broken statues, mannequins in absurd postures, clothes hanging on iron hooks, all create a fossilized symphony in the color tones of ash, earth, rotting greenery, and coagulated blood, with a few sepulchral-white splotches here and there. There must be an entrance, but where it might be is difficult to say.

The characters will enter by crawling out on all fours from beneath an old divan, or by appearing high up on a balcony, or by springing from the trap doors like jack-in-the-boxes. When they exit, they choose equally strange paths: passing through a wardrobe or climbing up a rope ladder. Pale rays of light filter down from dusty skylights hidden among the arches of the vaulted ceiling.

Keeping in mind the catacombs and Piranesi's engravings, the set designer will have to plan, in collaboration with the director, the appropriate devices that will make this huge machine practicable—and in the most surprising ways.

As the curtain opens, Isaac *is downstage to the left; he is busy examining some scraps of a fur coat disinterred from a large chest. Wearing a long slate-gray coat, shabby and threadbare, he may be obese or very skinny (depending on the physique of the actor), but his face must be opaque with sad yet resolute eyes; his hands are knotty and his hair and beard stringy.*

Downstage to the right, lying on a rug like an odalisque, Ariadne *is dealing out a game of solitaire with tarot cards. She is a young and beautiful woman, with an expressive face. At times she is animated but with something ambiguous in her way of laughing, then suddenly she will get a faraway look in her eyes and retreat into her own private world. She*

103

speaks and gestures slowly, moving like a lazy cat. If one of her breasts slips out from the décolletage of her pink and silver–flowered house robe, she nonchalantly replaces it. As the curtain opens she is half-heartedly humming the long, drawn-out, melancholy notes of a gypsy song.

Isaac. I'd give a year of my life to know where it is.

Ariadne. A year? Are you sure you have that much?

Isaac. Weren't those fur collars in here?

Ariadne. [*Laying out the cards.*] Queen, Emperor, Tower, and Merchant . . .

Isaac. [*Grumbling.*] This damned cavern! The more I look for things the less I find . . . There is nothing but disorder.

Ariadne. [*Placidly.*] Do you think it is any different outside?

Isaac. Outside where?

Ariadne. Outside in the world.

Isaac. I don't give a damn about what happens outside . . . The world goes its way, and I go mine.

Ariadne. Well, I think about it every once in a while. [*Dreamily.*] The seasons, for example . . . Rain, the sun, clouds . . . the wind, like a great skirt with its silken rustlings. And the swallows in springtime . . . the dusty streets, all violet down below and farther up flaked with ice crystals. And away in the distance the blue ribbon of the sea.

Isaac. You would do better to think about the shop.

Ariadne. [*Still in a dreamy voice.*] You once told me that your father used to go around with a little cart, buying and selling.

Isaac. So?

Ariadne. Nothing . . . But he must have seen the heat lightning in summer . . . women dancing beneath the lanterns . . . he would have heard the frogs croaking in the ditches.

Isaac. Yes, but you can't buy and sell that. You think about keeping our merchandise in order, mending clothes, and gluing broken pottery. That's what I pay you for.

Ariadne. [*Ironically.*] Yes, master.

Isaac. [*Angrily.*] And don't call me master! If I were master, I'd beat you.

Ariadne. Well, what should I call you? My little sweetie pie? And then what would happen if I slipped and said that in front of one of the customers?

Isaac. Don't be cute. Someday the real Master will come and I'll tell him everything and you'll be punished in the everlasting fire.

Ariadne. Well, I have some things to tell him, too.

Isaac. Really? He ought to get a good laugh out of that.

Ariadne. I don't think so. [*Mumbles as she lays out more cards.*] Sword and poison, letter and betrayal, flowered balcony and moonbeam . . . [*With a slight smile.*] And there is love's apprentice . . . [*Frowns.*] What is this card? . . . Isaac, do you know this card?

Isaac. [*Grumbling, he goes over to her and glances at the card.*] Where did you find it?

Ariadne. I don't know . . . It just now turned up.

Isaac. [*Takes the card and puts on his glasses to see it better.*] A guy with goat hooves . . . [*Gives it back.*] I don't like him . . . [*Returns to his chest.*] You must have mixed two different decks.

Ariadne. I tell you I didn't . . . [*Lays the card aside with a grimace of distaste.*] A guy with goat hooves . . .

Isaac. [*Continuing to rummage in the chest, he pulls out an old pair of shoes.*] Why, what are these doing in with the furs?

Ariadne. Maybe they were cold.

Isaac. The shoes?

Ariadne. Yes, the shoes . . . I heard them walking about last night. Now I know where they were going.

Isaac. [*Between his teeth.*] You are the one who walks about at night, leading your lovers around.

Ariadne. What lady does not accompany her guests?

A Voice. [*Distant and muffled.*] Hello . . . Hello . . .

Ariadne. [*In a loud voice but not ruffled.*] Who's there?

Isaac. Who do you think? Another one of those imbeciles who thought he was taking a shortcut and now doesn't know how to get out. [*Takes from the chest an astrakhan hat.*] Incredible! A hat, of all things!

Ariadne. [*Scarcely turning to look.*] It's fur, isn't it?

Isaac. [*Angrily.*] If I found a dead rat in here, you would say it was fur! [*The jumbled noises and the muffled shouts grow nearer and louder, as if someone were struggling with heaps of junk that block his path; finally, crawling on all fours, Chanusky emerges from a tunnel. He is bald and wrinkled, with protruding ears and lively eyes. His oversized clothes hang on him loosely. He looks like a sad and slightly frightened clown.*]

Chanusky. [*In a choking voice.*] At last! I didn't think I was going to make it. [*He gets up, coughs, tries to dust off his pants and pick off the cobwebs.*] It was all I could do to get out with my life! And the sign said: "Please come in." Now I understand. It's like the piece of cheese in a mousetrap.

Isaac. [*Without even looking at him.*] What are you yelling about?

Chanusky. I've been going up and down stairs, crossing balconies, climbing over piles of furniture . . . [*Looks at his suit.*] My clothes are so torn, it looks like I've been through a briar patch.

Isaac. You just lack a sense of direction, that's all!

Chanusky. You think it's easy to find your way in this labyrinth? [*Continues to clean himself off.*] Aisles that lead nowhere, ramps going up and down, ladders, trapdoors, grates.

Ariadne. Well, what do you think the signs are for?

Chanusky. Yeah, let's talk about those signs . . . Hands with six fingers . . . Adorable curve ahead . . . Even red arrows.

Ariadne. [*Smiling.*] That's because the electric wires run through there.

Chanusky. What about the obscene graffiti on the walls?

Ariadne. Those are compliments dedicated to me.

Chanusky. Ah!

Ariadne. Written by customers who are too shy to say them in person.

Chanusky. That's a nice way of doing things.

Isaac. [*With his head in the chest.*] Are you going to tell me what you want?

Chanusky. Are you the owner?

Isaac. [*Continuing to rummage about.*] Where the hell can it be? [*To the woman.*] Ariadne! You've been messing around in here, haven't you? Tell me the truth.

Ariadne. Do you think I want to catch leprosy? I'd have to be crazy! [*To* Chanusky.] You think those are fur pieces? They are lepers' beards.

Isaac. [*Angrily.*] You're the only leper around here!

Chanusky. [*To* Isaac.] Have you lost something?

Isaac. A beaver collar. It was right here. It's always been here. [*Shows a file card.*] It's even on the list: astrakhan, marten, and beaver trimmings. [*Snorts.*] Well, let it go. It will turn up eventually.

Chanusky. [*In a conciliatory voice.*] That's the way life is. You look and look and then one day . . .

Isaac. [*Brusquely.*] Yes, yes . . . Well, what's your problem?

Chanusky. [*Ceremoniously.*] My name is Chanusky . . . Peter Chanusky.

Isaac. I didn't ask you your name. What do you want?

Chanusky. Well, it's kind of hard to say . . . You might say that I need some advice.

Isaac. I don't carry that in stock.

Chanusky. Then let's say that I need some information.

Isaac. Are you with the police?

Chanusky. [*With a bitter smile.*] You must be joking. True, I do know all the police in Europe . . . those in uniform and in plain clothes, the mounted police and those on the beat, the ones with moustaches and those without.

Isaac. [*With a sidelong glance.*] International thief?

Chanusky. No . . . concentration camps, work camps, refugee camps. [*He pauses.*] I am an apolyde. Do you know what that means?

Isaac. [*Gruffly.*] More or less.

Chanusky. My country . . . my Fatherland, if you prefer big words . . . was cancelled from the map. [*Slashes the air with his hand.*] Zic! Zac! It's gone.

Ariadne. [*Picks up the cards and lays them out in a different way.*] Was it in some other country's way?

Chanusky. Yes, it was an obstacle. So we were deported in cattle cars like beasts. Scattered to the winds, turned back at every frontier, deprived of our civil rights. No longer men, but things . . . objects with a number. And all around us . . . guards and barbed wire. [*To* Isaac.] Do you know why? Can you tell me why?

Isaac. It was worse for us.

Chanusky. For you?

Ariadne. His name is Isaac.

Chanusky. Oh, I see . . . Gas chambers and crematory ovens.

Isaac. Can *you* tell me why?

Chanusky. Well . . . because intelligence is a threat to the powerful. A thief you can throw in jail; a murderer too. But intelligence? That you've got to burn at the stake. It's always been like that.

Ariadne. Maybe they're right. Intelligence is incorrigible.

Chanusky. It can't be confiscated, and it can be handed down to one's descendents without paying any inheritance tax.

Isaac. [*Waving a kind of scraggly tail that he has finally dug out of the chest.*] Here's the beaver collar! I knew it had to be there.

Chanusky. Ah, wonderful! That is most elegant. Congratulations! What is it good for?

Isaac. What do you mean, what's it good for? A beaver collar is the perfect thing to decorate a cashmere overcoat. One like that customer was wearing. [*Looking around the ladders and balconies.*] I wonder where he went to? [*Angrily.*] Ariadne, answer me!

Ariadne. How should I know where he went? [*To* Chanusky.] People come in here, they look for what we don't have, they ask for things that can't be found.

Chanusky. And they go away.

Ariadne. Of course not. They stay here like souls in purgatory. They climb up and down the ladders, poke around everywhere, complain.

Chanusky. Complain?

Ariadne. They cry, too.

Chanusky. You can't hear them from outside.

Ariadne. [*Indicating with a gesture the cavernous hall.*] It's a trap stuffed with old rags.

Isaac. [*Throwing the strip of fur into the chest.*] First they beg on their knees. That guy who wanted the beaver collar, for example, you would have thought that he couldn't live without it. He begged me to do everything possible to find it. He'd pay any price. Then . . . [*blowing on the palm of his hand*] pftt . . .

Chanusky. He disappeared?

Isaac. He left. [*With a vague gesture.*] *He* wanted to look for it. [*Shakes his head.*] Everybody thinks they are going to make a rare find. They dig around in the warehouse like it was a mine, looking for the most absurd things.

Chanusky. [*As though to himself.*] We all seek what can't be found.

Ariadne. [*To* Isaac.] But you know that people come here to look for what other merchants don't have. You ought to be proud.

Isaac. [*Grumbling.*] But they don't even know what they want.

Chanusky. Were you really so fond of that guy?

Ariadne. [*Laughing.*] He was his customer. Isaac gets infatuated with them.

Chanusky. I see . . . a serious buyer, who appreciates the merchandise. But I guess that women customers are more superficial.

Ariadne. [*Who has got up and lit a cigarette.*] No, there's no difference. Men or women, all of them are constantly searching for the impossible, urged on by who knows what anxieties, bitten by a nameless demon.

Isaac. [*To* Chanusky.] And they never tell you everything. Half sentences, disconnected words . . . It's hard to guess what secret desires are inside them. [*Slight pause.*] That guy looking for the beaver collar, for example . . . [*Makes a gesture of impatience.*] Oh, why am I always talking about him?

Chanusky. [*Looking around and talking to himself.*] They wander about in a cemetery . . . objects polished by the hands of whole generations, worn out by human toil, dried up by the years . . . Tired clothes, sick furniture, the fragments of lives long past.

Isaac. But when they come to sell, ah! They're sharp then. Every old rag is transformed into brocade, damask, silken velvet.

Every broken-down chair is a king's throne, every fragment a relic. The nobles are the worst of all, or those who call themselves nobles. You should see how their junk becomes manna from heaven. They weep over every bit of worm-eaten damask.

Chanusky. [*Still to himself.*] They sell their last illusions, they bargain away the remains of their shipwrecks . . . [*A silence.*]

Isaac. Well, are you going to tell me what you're looking for? In my shop we don't deal in talk; either we get down to business, or you leave.

Chanusky. Leave? That is out of the question. After all the meandering that I had to go through to get here?

Isaac. Don't worry. Ariadne will show you the shortest way out. [*Grumbling as he straightens some junk on a shelf.*] But what do you expect? Every year our stock grows, and we have to open new paths for the merchandise that piles up. We can't expand any more upstairs. We have to dig out new space in the basement. Who's to blame if it gets harder and harder to move around?

Ariadne. [*Smiling, to* Chanusky.] And then he is surprised when he can't find a beaver collar in this bedlam.

Isaac. I'm not surprised. Things are never where they are supposed to be, customers slip away from me like eels. Or else they don't tell me what they want. [*To* Chanusky.] You, for instance, what are you looking for?

Chanusky. Me? I . . . I would like a . . . prize.

Isaac. [*Surprised.*] A prize?

Chanusky. Yes, a prize.

Isaac. For having got into my store?

Chanusky. Why, no. What's got into you? Just a prize . . . for no reason.

Isaac. And you expect me to give it to you?

Chanusky. I don't know who I want to give it to me. Is there a central office for all the trouble that I have been through? And why should the prize come from there? [*Deliriously.*] But there has to be some kind of balance . . . Actually, logically, I should not even have to request the prize, just as I never asked for the misfortunes, the insults, the humiliations. But since the world is not perfect, I have decided to take the initiative. [*Gradually growing more excited.*] And I will get my prize! I have to have it! I can't die like this, become food for worms without ever having had anything. [*In a firm and dignified voice.*] I demand it, demand it, do you understand? A prize! A prize will make up for all I have suffered.

Isaac. My dear sir, you forget that you are only matter.

Chanusky. That may be so . . . but I am human, I am the matter that constitutes a living man.

Isaac. I know. And therefore you are an incomplete creature. A disharmony, a mistake. If I weren't afraid of offending you, well, I would call you a monstrosity.

Chanusky. [*Mortified.*] I am as my father made me. Perhaps he was a bit absentminded.

Isaac. [*Pressing his point.*] And the father of your father, was he, too, absentminded?

Chanusky. I can't go all the way back to the beginning.

Isaac. You must go back to the beginning. And you will find the Master. It's with him that you have to settle accounts.

Chanusky. What master?

Isaac. The one who made the first puppet . . . out of mud, naturally. He looked at it from all angles, then he said: "Well, it didn't turn out the way I had hoped, but it's too late now . . ." He breathed life into its nostrils and then off he went about his other business.

Chanusky. Breathed into its nostrils?

Isaac. That's what Genesis says.

Chanusky. [*Reflects for a minute.*] You just may be right. But that was his first model . . . You can't expect it to be perfect.

Isaac. And do you know why the Lord made only that one model? To preserve peace. So that no man, later, could say to another man, I am from a more advanced race than you. [*Solemnly.*] It's written in the Talmud.

Chanusky. [*Timidly.*] Don't you think that the puppet, in time, might improve?

Isaac. [*Shrugging his shoulders.*] For thousands of years the waves have beat upon the reefs, and they fall back shattered into spray that the sand reabsorbs. Each new crest thinks it is the strongest, the breaker that will smash everything. Illusions!

Chanusky. Then the Lord messed up the whole business?

Isaac. How should I know? Maybe men just haven't understood things yet . . . Maybe at the root of everything there is a mistake, a misunderstanding. It's not up to me to judge. When he comes, he will explain it to us.

Chanusky. [*Perplexed.*] When he comes?

Ariadne. [*Smiles.*] Didn't I tell you his name is Isaac?

Chanusky. [*To* Isaac.] Oh, yes . . . You're still waiting for him.

Isaac. [*Just a little sadly.*] We're all waiting for him, in one way or another.

Chanusky. With hope?

Isaac. Both hope and fear, just like the servants that we are. [*High* up in the balconies, a loud noise is heard. Maybe a pile of stools has fallen over. The three look up.]

Moko. [*A thin young black man comes to the railing holding a red jacket in his hands.*] Here it is! And you said you didn't have one . . .

Isaac. That's a jacket for lion tamers. You asked me for a jazz player's jacket.

Moko. [*Looks at the jacket.*] What's the difference?

Isaac. [*Furiously.*] The lion-tamer's jacket is double-breasted with black braid, the jazz player's jacket is single-breated with gold or silver buttons.

Moko. Can't you take off the braid and put buttons on?

Isaac. [*Shrugging his shoulders.*] You can do anything, but there's a service charge, naturally. Don't forget that the double breast has to be altered.

Moko. I'll pay the service charge. The important thing is that I have found what I wanted . . . It's a good thing that I insisted on rummaging around in all these corners.

Isaac. You didn't happen to run into that guy who wanted the beaver collar?

Moko. [*Still turning the red jacket over in his hands.*] The guy who wanted what?

Isaac. [*Shouting.*] The beaver collar, damn it! A short little fellow, with a bowler hat and a cashmere coat.

Moko. Was he wearing checkered pants?

Isaac. [*Snorting.*] I don't remember if he had checkered pants.

Moko. Well, a guy with checkered pants, I think I saw him around somewhere. [*Makes a vague gesture.*]

Isaac. [*To* Chanusky, *despairingly.*] Did you hear that? Somewhere . . . As if that was information.

Chanusky. [*Almost as though excusing Moko.*] We know so little about other people . . . But then, we know so little about ourselves.

Ariadne. [*To* Moko.] Well, are you going to come down here? That is the only way we'll be able to alter the jacket.

Moko. How do I get down?

Ariadne. [*Gathering up the cards and shuffling them.*] Go to your left; you'll find a ladder there; on the first landing you will find a sign with an arrow . . . Go in the opposite direction.

Moko. Away from the arrow?

Ariadne. Away from the arrow, yes . . . still keeping to your right, take the third passageway to the left. You'll see an arch with two sabers over it. You can't miss it.

Moko. Okay. [*He moves away uncertainly and disappears mumbling.*] To the left . . . a ladder . . . sign with an arrow.

Ariadne. [*To* Isaac.] Do you want to bet that he takes a wrong turn?

Isaac. He can go to the devil, him and his jacket!

Ariadne. [*To* Chanusky, *smiling.*] He doesn't like him.

Chanusky. Who?

Ariadne. The black. There are some people that Isaac likes and some that he doesn't.

Chanusky. [*Timidly.*] Do you think he'll like me?

Ariadne. How should I know? In any case, don't hope for any prize from him. All he thinks about is buying and selling.

Chanusky. He also thinks about the Lord . . . He is waiting for him.

Ariadne. [*Impatiently.*] He has been waiting for him for thousands of years.

Chanusky. What about you?

Ariadne. [*Shrugs her shoulders.*] What does it matter?

Chanusky. [*Anxiously.*] Hope, I mean . . . a new day, with a sun that casts real light, with dreams that have come true and illusions that are believable . . . Maybe no more defeats.

Ariadne. [*Doubtfully.*] And love, too?

Chanusky. Love, yes . . . and justice for all. Life no longer bogged down in sand, no longer any emptiness as heavy as a tombstone, no more sealed sacks or gags or slip knots. [*He stops, panting; then, as though in a trance.*] To finally feel inside yourself something . . . indestructible.

Ariadne. [*Seized by a sudden memory.*] When I was a little girl I used to live next to an oil refinery . . . A big squat building with a tall smokestack that blackened the sky with smoke during the day and at night flamed like a torch blowing in the wind. Everything tasted like oil, even the bread and the water; but not to us, only to those who came from outside . . . We could eat oil and be happy . . .

Chanusky. [*Talking to himself.*] Me, I am inside and outside at the same time. I can't see myself with the eyes of others or smell myself with the nose of others; but I contemplate my damnation, and I breathe in the rancid odor of a man who is done for.

Moko. [*Appears on the balcony.*] I've got this far.

Ariadne. [*Angrily.*] You are impossible! Why don't you keep going?

Moko. Keep going where?

Ariadne. Turn around! Isn't there a ramp behind you? A ramp going down?

Moko. [*Turning around.*] A ramp, yeah, I see it.

Ariadne. At the bottom there is a landing, and if you turn to the right you'll see . . .

Moko. . . . myself.

Ariadne. What?

Moko. Yeah . . . Three times now I have run into a mirror, and I think it is somebody else. But it is just me.

Isaac. It wouldn't have been, by any chance, that short little fellow with the bowler hat and the cashmere coat?

Moko. [Irritated.] What do you mean, a short little fellow? I see myself with my long arms and legs and my black face . . . my awful black face.

Ariadne. [Smiling.] Why awful? You're a good-looking man; you ought to like to look at yourself in the mirror.

Moko. Well, I don't; because I see myself different from what I want to be, even from what I am.

Ariadne. But aren't you black?

Moko. [Angrily.] No! I was born in America. And my father was born in America and my grandfather, too.

Ariadne. And I was hoping that you would tell me some beautiful stories about Africa . . . with palm trees and deserts . . . and women in veils and camels.

Moko. [Vexed.] Yeah, you're not the first one. Every once in a while I meet somebody who says: "Tell me about Africa . . ." What Africa? I've never seen it.

Chanusky. [In a conciliatory tone of voice.] But that's an understandable mistake. You carry Africa around with you, without knowing it.

Moko. I don't give a damn about mistakes. It's the contempt . . . I know that it is a way of expressing contempt.

Chanusky. Well, it shouldn't be too hard to explain . . .

Moko. [Interrupting him.] Explain what? Have you ever been able to explain yourself? What words did you use? *[Pauses, then as though to himself.]* And all the while your soul grows old inside you, it is humiliated, it hides . . . *[A silence, then Moko runs away as though in desperation, losing himself in the labyrinth of the warehouse, and we hear bits of dry harsh phrases like orders.]* Forward to the right! Left turn! A mirror . . . don't look!

Isaac. [Trying to call him back.] Wait a minute! If you meet that fellow who wants the beaver collar . . . *[Since Moko has disappeared, he drops his arms in discouragement, then turns to Chanusky.]* A customer who knew what he wanted, and I lost him.

Chanusky. [Absentmindedly.] Who?

Isaac. [Suddenly angry again.] The one with the cashmere coat!

Ariadne. [Beginning again to play solitaire.] Don't give up. When a customer really wants something, he always comes back.

Isaac. [Obsessed by one idea.] A beaver collar that was a real bargain.

Chanusky. Do you believe in real bargains?

Ariadne. He believes in everything. In the Master who is supposed
   to come, in customers who are passing by and come in just to
   look around or to waste a little time and cause us to waste it, too.
Chanusky. Do many people come in?
Ariadne. Yes. [*Pause.*] You don't think that there is anyone here, do
   you? They sneak in, poke about, sniff around like dogs. If you
   listen, you'll always hear someone rummaging about, scratching
   around . . . even at night, and it's not mice.
Chanusky. Could they just be lost?
Ariadne. That, too.
Chanusky. And useless people? Lost souls?
Ariadne. Nobody is useless. Not to us, anyway. Where would we be
   without customers? Holidays, for instance, are terrible. They
   last forever. You may wonder why we are in here, what we are
   doing here . . . With customers we bargain, we even argue, and
   that makes us feel alive, it gives us the sensation of existing.
Chanusky. Do you like existing?
Ariadne. It's the only way we can feel ourselves to be human. Then
   death comes, which is the same for both men and animals; and
   that is why we fear it.
Isaac. [*To* Chanusky *in a confidential voice.*] There are also people
   who come here only to steal.
Chanusky. To steal what?
Isaac. [*Nods toward* Ariadne.] Her, for one thing . . . Shoulders,
   arms, legs . . . What they see and what they imagine.
Chanusky. And do you suffer?
Isaac. [*Sadly.*] Yes . . . [*Slight pause.*] But I don't dislike it, because
   this suffering is the proof of my virility.
Ariadne. [*With a shrill little laugh.*] You're talking nonsense.
Isaac. [*To* Chanusky, *smugly.*] Hear that? Just like a woman. Another proof . . .
A Man's Voice. [*From above.*] Excuse me? [*Two young men appear at the
   top of the central ladder; they are dressed in rustic garb: corduroy
   jackets and baggy pants. The older one,* Chalcedony, *has a haversack
   slung across his shoulders; the younger one,* Cosmo, *lugs a cheap fiber
   suitcase tied with a cord. The young man with the haversack is taller
   and more robust, and his face is tight-lipped and hard. The one with the
   suitcase, hardly out of adolescence, is all smiles.*]
Isaac. Come on down! [*To* Chanusky.] There is never a moment's
   peace.
Chalcedony. [*Greets everyone somewhat awkwardly as he comes down the
   ladder, followed by* Cosmo.] Can I speak to the boss?
Chanusky. [*Mutters as he watches the new arrivals.*] Everybody com-

plains about the lack of freedom, yet they're always looking for a boss.

Chalcedony. [*In a hollow voice as he puts down his haversack.*] You have a boss when you're born and a boss when you die. Freedom is for people who have money. No money, no freedom.

Ariadne. [*To* Chanusky, *smiling.*] They are from the South. [*To the two young men.*] Are you from the Island?

Cosmo. [*With a childlike smile.*] Yes, from the Island . . . Have you been there? We are right from its center, the interior . . . [*To* Isaac.] Woods and mountains . . .

Isaac. Bandits, too?

Cosmo. Well, there are a few of them left. But all they know is stealing. Can you steal the sun? Can you steal hunger?

Chalcedony. That's right. Sun and hunger. That's all we have on the Island.

Isaac. Earthquakes and despair.

Chalcedony. Yes, sir. Earthquakes, too; but no despair.

Cosmo. [*Gaily.*] Everybody hopes to find work . . . Take us, for example . . .

Chalcedony. [*Looks at the boy severely.*] What do you mean, "us"? [*Intimidated, the boy falls silent.*]

Isaac. Well, what do you want?

Chalcedony. My name is Chalcedony Niscemi. [*Points to the young boy.*] And this is my cousin, Cosmo; or rather he is my cousin-brother.

Isaac. What do you mean?

Chalcedony. We are the sons of two brothers who married two sisters.

Cosmo. [*Obviously satisfied.*] We are from the same town, and we live in the same house.

Ariadne. [*Smiling.*] So you also left home together?

Chalcedony. [*As if to justify himself.*] Cosmo has no one, no father or mother . . . So I said to him, you come with me, we'll find something for you to do.

Isaac. [*Grumbling.*] Well, if you're looking for work here, all our positions are filled.

Chalcedony. [*Ironically.*] Do you think we would have left our town just to work here? We want to go to America.

Ariadne. [*Amused.*] Oh, to America? Good for you. [*During the following dialogue, her eyes often meet* Cosmo's; *a pleasant surprise and also a slight confusion can be seen in their looks.*]

Cosmo. [*Enthusiastically.*] We have to catch a ship . . . one of these days.

Isaac. [*Snorts.*] Well, this is no seaport.

Chalcedony. Do you think we plan to leave from here? We want you to find us two sailor suits.

Cosmo. [*With childlike precision.*] Outfits for third-class seamen.

Chalcedony. We'll pay for them, naturally.

Chanusky. [*To* Isaac.] They plan to stow away.

Cosmo. [*Happily.*] Stow away, that's right . . . a guy from our home-town is supposed to help us. He's got an important job. He's a fireman on the ship. But to get on board we have to be dressed like sailors. That's what he told us.

Ariadne. But do you know how many days it takes to get to America?

Chalcedony. [*Tiredly.*] Days don't mean nothing when you've been suffering for years.

Chanusky. Listen . . . I've traveled a lot, even on ships, and I know what it is like to be shut up in the hold of a ship, maybe near the boilers. I've seen stowaways die, suffocated by the heat from the boilers . . . And then do you know what happens? They tie a piece of scrap iron to their feet and throw them to the sharks.

Chalcedony. [*Shrugging his shoulders.*] If they couldn't take it, they weren't men.

Cosmo. We are used to working in mines. Fifteen hundred feet below the earth, where it gets to be 110, even 120 degrees.

Ariadne. Under ground?

Cosmo. Yeah, digging sulfur.

Isaac. And do you think there are no miners in America? Do you think they are waiting just for you?

Chalcedony. [*With a superior smile.*] We're not going there to be miners.

Cosmo. [*Enthusiastically.*] Radio repairmen!

Chanusky. You are skilled workers?

Cosmo. [*Increasingly euphoric.*] Skilled? We are technicians. [*To* Chalcedony.] Show him the diploma!

Chalcedony. [*From his wallet he takes a dirty sheet of paper folded twice and hands it to* Chanusky.] Read it.

Chanusky. [*Reading*] Chalcedony Niscemi, son of Giuseppe. Diploma awarded in radio repair. The above-named person has successfully completed the course in radio repair from the Read-and-Do Correspondence School."

Chalcedony. [*Proudly.*] I had to study a whole year, and by mail, too. Three hundred lire for each lesson. And the Diploma cost me a thousand.

Cosmo. [*Touches his brother's elbow.*] Show him the instrument. [*To* Chanusky.] We even have an instrument . . .

Chalcedony. [*Takes a long screwdriver from his haversack and shows it around.*] Here it is!

Chanusky. A screwdriver?

Chalcedony. Yeah, Solid steel.

Ariadne. [*To* Cosmo.] What about you?

Cosmo. I help my brother. I'm an apprentice . . .

Ariadne. [*Bursts out laughing.*] An apprentice?

Cosmo. [*Also laughing.*] What's so funny? I'm an apprentice . . . [*Takes the screwdriver from his brother's hand.*] In fact, *I'm* supposed to carry this. [*Sticks it in his belt like a knife.*]

Chalcedony. [*Good-humoredly.*] That's right. [*To the others, as if to excuse him.*] He's just a boy . . .

Chanusky. And have you already repaired some radios?

Chalcedony. [*Vexed.*] How could we? There aren't any in our town. Only the baron has one, but he never uses it because his sister don't want him to waste electricity.

Cosmo. But in America everybody's got them. Even in their pockets . . . radios no bigger than a pack of cigarettes. Just think . . . maybe you're taking a trip on a train and you hear somebody talking. You look around, but nobody's moving their lips. Then you realize that the guy over there, the one reading a newspaper, maybe, has a radio in his pocket. [*Laughs childishly.*]

Ariadne. [*To* Isaac.] There are some radios here in the shop.

Isaac. [*Quickly.*] They are already in good repair! [*To* Chalcedony.] And we don't have any sailor suits. Or time to waste.

Ariadne. You leave the sailor suits to me.

Isaac. Where are you going to get them?

Ariadne. There are shelves full of blue cloth . . . I've got white ribbon, and there ought to be some striped shirts on the third floor . . . [*Smiles at Cosmo.*] I'll give *you* one with red stripes.

Isaac. [*Irritated.*] You're not going to start sewing navy uniforms, are you? That's all we need. [*To* Chalcedony.] Anyway, you fellows are probably looking for previously owned items.

Chalcedony. Previously owned?

Isaac. I mean used clothes . . . Those that don't cost much.

Chalcedony. [*Takes a few bills out of his pocket.*] I don't know what the prices run, but this is what I've got left. See if it is enough.

Cosmo. [*Takes a bottle of oil from the pocket of his hunting jacket.*] We've got this, too. [*To* Isaac.] Do you want it? It's good oil, made from real olives.

Ariadne. [*Refuses with a gesture.*] You can pay later. Come with me.

Isaac. Where are you taking them?

Ariadne. Well, they have to sleep somewhere, at least until tomor-

row. You can't just throw together two sailor uniforms. [*To*
Chalcedony.] When are you shipping out?

Chalcedony. When we get the signal.

Cosmo. Our buddy is supposed to send us word by one of his
friends. We have to wait until the last minute, when the ship is
set to leave. There is always a lot of confusion, people getting
on, people getting off . . . Do you see?

Ariadne. [*Smiling.*] I see . . . Let's go! [*She starts off, singing a gypsy
song at the top of her voice, and the emigrants follow her. At the end of
each refrain, the girl holds a long, sweet note, and she turns to look at*
Cosmo. *The three disappear high up. The song fades away in the
distance.*]

Isaac. [*To* Chanusky.] Do you think a business can make any
headway when it's run like this?

Chanusky. The girl is sensitive.

Isaac. [*Shrugging his shoulders.*] Not sensitive . . . sensual. That
woman is always in heat.

Chanusky. The Lord must have created her that way.

Isaac. Well, he did a poor job of it.

Chanusky. But you yourself said that the Lord made men incomplete. How can you expect him to have reached perfection
in woman?

Isaac. Yeah . . . Maybe he did it on purpose so we wouldn't forget
the burden of our flesh and our original sin.

Chanusky. Well, since we're on the subject, let me tell you that even
the hermits in the desert . . .

Isaac. [*Interrupts him.*] Nossir! They took refuge in the desert
because they weren't able to create a desert within themselves.

Chanusky. I was just trying to say . . .

Isaac. There is nothing to say. I don't like hermits . . . I never have.

Chanusky. And have you succeeded in creating a desert within
yourself?

Isaac. [*Grumbling.*] I would have, if my wife hadn't died and left me
with this whole warehouse on my back . . . I needed somebody
to help me out . . . in my business, of course.

Chanusky. [*Maliciously.*] So you ran a classified ad in the newspaper:
"Attractive salesgirl wanted."

Isaac. I didn't say "attractive" . . . Besides, that would have cost an
extra word.

Chanusky. But when the girl showed up, you didn't send her away.

Isaac. It was too late . . . The demon had already got hold of me.

[*The trapdoor clangs and the head of the* Reporter *appears; he looks
around with a listless eye, then he hoists himself up onto the floor huffing*

and wavering a little. He is a middle-aged man, in shirt sleeves. He has a loose, lanky build, a face the color of leather, and tiny eyes, with the jovial and good-natured manner of the inveterate drinker.]

Reporter. Good morning, gentlemen . . . Bonjour . . . [*Touches his forehead with two fingers.*] Am I interrupting anything?

Isaac. Customers never interrupt.

Reporter. Thank you, I'm sure . . . [*Pauses.*] What did you say?

Isaac. [*Shouting.*] That customers never interrupt . . . even if they've been drinking . . .

Reporter. [*Good-humoredly.*] Ah, yes, I have had a drink . . . Is there any other medicine for the soul?

Isaac. I am not a doctor . . . I am a businessman.

Reporter. So that's why you were talking about customers. Well, for your information, I too am a vendor.

Isaac. What do you sell?

Reporter. Words.

Isaac. Are you trying to be funny?

Reporter. Why should I? I am a journalist. I am a roving reporter— or a special correspondent, if you like that better.

Chanusky. [*Offers his hand.*] May I introduce myself? I am Cha- nusky . . . Peter Chanusky.

Reporter. Pleased to meet you. [*Shakes his hand.*] Are you a phi- latelist?

Chanusky. [*A bit surprised.*] No . . . an apolyde.

Reporter. Then we are contemporaries. [*Laughs.*] It's a joke, do you get it?

Isaac. [*To the* Reporter, *blustering.*] As you must have read on one of the signs at the entrance, we buy and sell here . . . But we don't buy words . . . We'd be in a fine fix if the only people who came in here were buyers of goods and sellers of words. In a few years we'd have to close up shop. We need tangible goods, measurable objects.

Ariadne. [*Who has reappeared, gracefully climbing out of a wardrobe.*] Isaac's great fear . . . To be left with nothing to sell . . . If he could, he would stick the moon and the stars in here—with a price tag, of course.

Reporter. [*Takes a flat bottle from the back pocket of his pants and drinks from it.*] He who accumulates is condemned to become a pris- oner of things. [*To Isaac, who is peering at the bottle.*] Anyway, I didn't see your signs.

Ariadne. Maybe you came in a side entrance.

Reporter. Could be.

Isaac. And as you passed through the cellar, you took a bottle.

Reporter. Why, yes .. I won't deny it. [*Takes another swig.*] The bottles were on a low shelf, right at my fingertips . . . I resisted for a minute, then, you know how it is . . . curiosity. [*Laughing.*] Let's see what's in that one . . . [*Changes his tone.*] Anyway, just consider it a foible, nothing but a foible.

Isaac. [*Coldly.*] I consider it a bottle of Jamaican rum, and it costs fifteen hundred lire.

Reporter. Okay, okay . . . I am a gentleman. [*Looks for money in all his pockets, then finally finds a few bills in a shoe.*] Here's your money . . .

Isaac. Thank you. Do you need anything else? We have compasses, maps of nonexistent countries, very useful, I believe, for journalists, explorers, and other world travelers.

Reporter. No, no . . . I need only a typewriter. My last one was confiscated for some stupid financial disagreement. [*Wiggles his fingers as if they were striking a keyboard.*] And without a typewriter I can't even think.

Chanusky. The typewriter thinks for you?

Reporter. It is a part of me. It inspires me, gets me started, sometimes even suggests an appropriate subject.

Chanusky. Like a piano for a musician.

Reporter. Even more so. I would ask it questions, and the typewriter would answer me. I would be sad and it would console me, I would be about to perish and I would find salvation by going to my typewriter, like a drowning man to a reef.

Chanusky. That's very convenient.

Reporter. You might say that. Since they took away my typewriter, I feel like an amputee.

Ariadne. [*Who has gone back to her solitaire.*] We've got several of them. Used ones, naturally.

Reporter. [*Lighting a cigarette.*] What kind?

Ariadne. All kinds. Extra-wide carriages, portables, hybrids . . . With Cyrillic characters, Chinese ideograms, even some with multicolored keys for dreamers and poets.

Isaac. Shall I show you some?

Reporter. No, I prefer to look around by myself. . . I believe in destiny, and I am sure that my typewriter already exists somewhere in this mausoleum of junk . . . It may have already learned of my arrival and is looking for me. [*With a start.*] Sssshh . . . Be quiet! [*Turns his head and listens.*] Do you hear? [*Far away can be heard the clacking of a typewriter, stereophonically amplified. The* Reporter *smiles and winks.*] There it is . . . I'm going to look for it. [*Climbs agilely up a rope ladder hanging from the ceiling and disappears.*]

Isaac. [*To* Chanusky.] See that? They're all like that . . . I could guide them around, give them advice. Nothing doing! *They* want to do it, *they* want to make the discovery. Then they get lost, beat on the exits, call for help.

Ariadne. And I have to track them down.

Chanusky. Presumption is a grave human failing.

Isaac. And to augment their arrogance they invented machines. . . .

Chanusky. But perhaps arrogance is a deceit, a trick to hide fear.

Isaac. [*Suspiciously.*] What's this about fear?

Ariadne. This is an impregnable fortress.

Chanusky. Even if everyone comes in, wanders about, snoops around?

Isaac. [*Vexed.*] Even if no one commands, and no one obeys.

Chanusky. [*Laughing.*] But when the Lord comes . . .

Isaac. I will tell Him to strike harder . . . [*Angrily.*] And still harder.

Chanusky. Do you think that he will come to punish?

Isaac. If he didn't, what kind of Lord would he be?

Chanusky. . . . [*He is about to answer but is prevented by the arrival of* Moko, *who comes crawling out on all fours from beneath a divan.*]

Moko. [*Waves his jacket as a sign of triumph.*] I've done it. Here I am! [*To* Ariadne.] But it's a good thing I didn't follow the directions on the signs.

Ariadne. Didn't you go away from the arrow?

Moko. No. I just wandered at random. When I came to an intersection I flipped a coin . . . [*Showing* Chanusky *the jacket.*] Nice looking, isn't it?

Chanusky. Volcano red.

Ariadne. Blood red.

Moko. Barricade red. [*Gives the jacket to the woman.*]

Chanusky. Bravo! Let me introduce myself . . . Chanusky . . . Peter Chanusky.

Moko. [*Shaking his hand.*] Very glad to meet you . . . Moko.

Chanusky. I suppose that's a stage name.

Moko. Thought up by my agent.

Chanusky. Are you a musician?

Moko. [*Jovially.*] A drummer . . . The beat that leads the orchestra. The insanity that runs along the lines of the music staff.

Chanusky. I see . . . Jazz?

Moko. Classical jazz, of course . . . Hot jazz.

Chanusky. At one time it didn't even exist . . . at least in my country.
Moko. [*Absentmindedly.*] Yeah . . . Adagio, pianissimo, allegretto ma non troppo . . .
Chanusky. [*Smiling.*] Andantino, grave, lento, maestoso . . .
Moko. But today, shouts, invectives, joy and despair. [*As if to himself.*] And the drums beat a tattoo, a muted grumble, they argue, bite, let loose, gallop away, and shatter into glasslike fragments . . . Then suddenly they stop, and the hall grows silent . . . The dancers are motionless statues . . . The world has stopped in space.
Chanusky. Do you play in a nightclub?
Moko. Yes, at the Crazy Bat, a second-class dive. From quarter after ten in the evening to half past two in the morning.
Chanusky. [*Rubs his thumb and index finger together.*] Does it pay well?
Moko. Not bad . . . But the doctors eat up everything I earn and I've gone into debt buying medicine.
Ariadne. Are you sick?
Moko. Not at all. I'm as healthy as a horse, but I want to be white, and whitening specialists cost.
Ariadne. What kind of treatment do they give you?
Moko. A little of everything . . . Calcified vitamins, Swedish hormones, ultraopaline rays, bleaching baths, hyperemicizing massages.
Chanusky. Have they done any good?
Moko. [*Points.*] My hair, which used to be kinky, is straight now, see? But they haven't been able to change my skin color much. Except here, around my ears; if you look closely, you'll see a kind of paleness. The specialist explained to me that the subcutaneous pigment first has to carbonize, then it gets white. It just takes time . . . The aesthetic therapist says that my pigmentation is unusually recalcitrant. It's not absorbing the ultraopaline rays.
Chanusky. Well, don't take it too hard. I'm white, and it happens to me, too.
Moko. What do you mean?
Chanusky. I don't have any luck in getting absorbed. As soon as a city swallows me up, it immediately spits me out like a bone. All my life has been one long battle to get settled somewhere.
Moko. Why don't you go live in the country?
Chanusky. There is no more country . . . It's just scattered cities now, with machines that plow and reap, farmers dressed like mechanics, and radio and television in all the farmhouses.

[*Pauses, then to himself.*] Maybe up in the mountains . . . The big ones with caves and wolves . . . But I'll go there afterward . . .

Moko. After what?

Chanusky. After I get my prize.

Moko. Are you expecting a prize?

Chanusky. I demand one, sir. [*Pauses, then in a kind of lucid delirium.*] Now you're going to tell me that I have to earn it. But who judges, who decides, who takes the initiative in giving out prizes? Have you ever wondered about that?

Moko. Well, I guess . . .

Chanusky. [*Without giving him time to answer.*] Well, you guess wrong. No one will ever give you a prize if you don't ask for it. [*Brief pause.*] Six years of war on every front . . . And do you think that anyone ever even shook my hand? Five years behind barbed wire . . . Do you think that anyone ever asked himself: "What's that poor guy over there doing?" [*Mimics the scene.*] "The last one in line . . . yeah, that's the one, the bald guy with the jug ears . . . [*he hunches over*] that man all stooped over, holding his mess tin. [*Wriggles around like an eel.*] And why does everybody laugh when the soldier kicks him?" [*In his normal tone of voice.*] Do you think anybody ever said that? And there are thousands and thousands of miserable wretches like me in the world, all in the same boat because of the massive indifference of the prize givers. [*Brief pause.*] Then one day I understood. If you want a prize you have to ask for it imperiously, just like all those who don't deserve one do. [*A banging is heard from above, as though someone were knocking on a door, while a woman's muffled voice implores: "Open up! Open up!"*]

Isaac. Looks like somebody got trapped in the dead-end passage!

Ariadne. [*Going toward a ladder.*] Not again! Why, there is even a sign that says: "Dead-end corridor" . . . I think they do it on purpose! [*She reappears on the first balcony and raises a small rolling shop-shutter. Immediately, as though sliding off a toboggan, Tanya jumps out. She is a middle-aged woman, with wide eyes, wirelike hair, and a body that shakes as though it is about to shatter into pieces. Tanya is wearing an elegant, tobacco-colored nineteenth-century gown with elaborate decorations of ivory-white lace.*]

Tanya. [*Panting.*] Air, air . . . [*She leans her back against the railing and, still terrified, stares at the rolling shop-shutter.*] I almost suffocated to death . . . Now I know what it means to be buried alive. Horrible! Horrible!

Ariadne. [*Returning to the first floor.*] Don't exaggerate. It is only a corridor that is a little bit narrow because of the algae: it swells up when it gets damp. [*To* Isaac.] I don't know what we are ever going to do with that dried algae . . . That was a bad deal. But you would even buy potato peelings, if the price was right.

Tanya. [*Melodramatically.*] A long sepulcher lined with slimy tentacles . . . Octopus and jellyfish, beaks and suckers . . . [*She suddenly turns and sees* Chanusky.] Peter, Peter, at last!

Chanusky. [*With a sigh.*] Yes, Tanya.

Tanya. I have been looking for you, praying for you since yesterday . . . [*She slides to her knees, her hands gripping the railing.*] Milord, kill me, take me with you, I can't stand it any longer.

Isaac. [*To* Tanya.] Look, this is a business establishment, not a court for marital disputes.

Tanya. You don't understand, sir . . . Ten years of torment, ten years . . .

Chanusky. [*To* Isaac.] She's insane. I've never laid a hand on her. Not even one finger.

Tanya. [*In the same melodramatic voice.*] Better if you had beaten me, tortured me, even killed me, rather than stifle my desires for a dignified and harmonious life. [*She turns slightly to the others.*] It's no use! He doesn't see me . . . Both of us are in a fog . . . I sometimes catch myself speaking in sign language, like a deaf-mute.

Isaac. [*Very irritated.*] Unfortunately, you are not a deaf-mute, but you are disrupting my business.

Tanya. [*Quivering.*] Ah, you're in business? What kind of business? Fleas and cockroaches? Condemned men's clothes and dead mice? [*She points to* Ariadne.] And is she for sale, too?

Ariadne. [*Placidly.*] No, madam, I give myself away. Instead of making a discount on the merchandise, the company offers me to its customers, as a bonus.

Tanya. [*To* Chanusky.] And you frequent a place like this? With not even one word for me? While I have been desperately looking for you, running like a crazed mole through a labyrinth of corridors, stairs, balconies . . . But not a single thought for your wife walled up in algae-filled tombs . . . your poor wife who drags her misery through fog peopled with shadows and phantoms.

Isaac. [*With a sigh.*] I don't suppose that in your wanderings you would have run across a short little guy with a bowler hat and a cashmere overcoat?

Tanya. No, sir, I have not seen him. My eyes are weak from weeping. I am a nervous wreck, almost exhausted. Ten years of traipsing across Europe in the wake of this man, with never a home, never the possibility of acquiring a solid identity and of being elected to the women's auxiliary.

Chanusky. [*To* Isaac, *disconsolately.*] At last she has confessed it! The women's auxiliary! . . . Like her mother, like her grandmother . . . An auxiliary by hereditary right! [*To* Tanya *with a sudden outburst.*] And what does home mean? Iron and concrete? Glass and locks? Working just so one can survive physically? [*Shouting.*] I want no part of it! I refuse! I have been uprooted from proper society, and I don't want to go back to it. [*He grows increasingly agitated; then he turns to* Isaac.] Order frightens me, the charity doled out by the women's auxiliary is repugnant to me . . . And the judges enshrined in their robes, have you ever seen them? And the scientists who rape the cosmos and subvert molecular equilibrium in order to hasten the Apocalypse? Because if you accept the home, you have to accept all the rest . . . the truth of the courtroom instead of real truth, the government's reason instead of logic . . . It is a machine, a terrible machine.

Reporter. [*Coming to the balcony.*] Pardon me . . . Please excuse me.

Isaac. Did you find your typewriter?

Reporter. Yes, it's wonderful. As soon as I touched the keys it wrote me a love letter.

Isaac. [*Clapping his hands.*] Then we're in business! [*Shouting.*] Ariadne! Go get the typewriter that the gentleman has chosen and bring it here.

Ariadne. [*Rising lazily.*] Right away. [*She goes upstairs humming and disappears in the labyrinth of stairs and balconies.*]

Moko. [*To* Isaac.] What about my jacket?

Isaac. Don't worry. Ariadne will remove the braid and sew on the silver buttons. Would you like some chevrons on the sleeves, too?

Moko. That would be nice.

Isaac. Gold epaulets?

Moko. [*He smiles in embarrassment.*] You are tempting me.

Isaac. I've got a beautiful pair of them, and I'll let them go at a good price.

Moko. [*Shaking* Isaac's *hand.*] All right, the epaulets, too.

Isaac. You won't regret it.

Moko. So I can leave?

Isaac. Yes, and by tonight you will have the jacket with silver buttons, chevrons on the sleeves, and gold epaulets.

Moko. Thank you . . . How do I get out?

Isaac. Ariadne will show you. [*Shouting.*] Ariadne! [*He pauses, then to* Moko.] There may be a short delay, she's probably making love with that reporter.

Moko. I hope they hurry.

Chanusky. [*To* Isaac.] Is Ariadne the only one who knows the exits?

Isaac. She knows a lot of them . . . But not all of them, of course. There are still unexplored corridors, galleries that connect up with the sewers of the city, grottoes that have been carved by erosion . . . And then the cave-ins.

Chanusky. There is a danger of landslides, too?

Isaac. Not *land*slides—cave-ins of furniture, scrap paper, old rags. As the merchandise accumulates, the center of gravity shifts away from the perimeter of the base, understand? And then everything topples over, comes down, caves in . . . It takes days, weeks, months to hack out a passageway with a hatchet.

Moko. So even when *you* want to go out . . .

Isaac. Ah, I never go out. I've got used to staying in here day and night, ever since the war.

Chanusky. You're like a cockroach.

Issac. Well, is it the poor bug's fault if, as soon as he goes out into the light, there is a shoe ready to squash him? And why should *I* go out? All my generation is dead. I feel closer to them living here under the ground.

Chanusky. But others have been born. The cities have grown, there are no more blackouts, the streets are filled with crowds.

Isaac. [*Raising his arms.*] For the love of God, don't tell me about crowds. That scum stuck together with selfishness and cowardice horrifies and disgusts me. Have the crowds ever lifted a finger to save an innocent person? The crowds go to church, to football games, to wars. That is all they are good for. The crowd is an obscene animal—when it is not being a ferocious beast.

Ariadne. [*She appears with an ancient typewriter in her arms.*] Here's the sucker bait.

Isaac. I've told you a thousand times not to joke about the merchandise.

Reporter. [*Who has come in behind* Ariadne.] Don't worry, I adore sucker bait. [*He takes the typewriter from the girl's arms and carefully lays it on the large chest.*] Do you have a dust rag?

Isaac. You can clean it easier at home. It would be useless to do it here, there is dust everywhere. [*To* Ariadne, *as he points to* Moko.] In the meantime, show the gentleman the way out.

Ariadne. [*To* Moko.] Follow me, please.

Chanusky. Do you have any objections if I come, too?

Ariadne. Not at all. Come along.

Tanya. [*From up in the balcony.*] Just a minute . . . I'm leaving, too.

Ariadne. [*Dryly.*] I'll lead out who I please and when I please! [*She turns to the right, draws aside a screen and uncovers a passageway; she enters it, followed by the two men.* Tanya *begins screaming and running from one balcony to another.*]

Tanya. Help! Help! Let me out! You don't want to aid and abet kidnapping. Peter! Peter! [*She disappears among the drapings of rags, though her shouts continue for a little while, far off.*]

Isaac. [*To* the Reporter.] Is this any way to run a business? Now you tell me. And every day things like this happen.

Reporter. [*Carefully dusting the typewriter with his handkerchief.*] Humanity is becoming more and more frantic . . . maybe we are heading for a collective insanity . . . Nature's wonderful foresight, so that we won't even be aware of the end of the world. [*Pause.*] How much do I owe you for this thing?

Isaac. [*He goes to read the tag hanging from the carriage return lever.*] Well, let's see . . . S, C, M, zero, zero. [*He goes to an abacus and after moving the beads around, he exclaims.*] Ten thousand.

Reporter. Couldn't you knock a little bit off that?

Isaac. It's against company policy; but I'll tell you what, I'll throw in a bottle of bootleg brandy.

Reporter. Hey, you're all right.

Ariadne. [*With* Moko *and* Chanusky *at her side, she appears on one of the upstairs balconies and shouts.*] Isaac!

Isaac. [*Raising his head.*] What's the matter?

Ariadne. We can't get out.

Isaac. Another cave-in?

Ariadne. Cave-in, my foot. There are guards at all the exits.

Isaac. Are they armed?

Ariadne. To the teeth. And they want a password. The whole neighborhood is blocked off.

Isaac. When did all this happen?

Ariadne. A half hour ago. That's what the guy in the bowler hat told me.

Isaac. Ah, so you finally found him?

Ariadne. Well, in a way I did. They have taken him as a hostage.

Reporter. [*Still busy cleaning his typewriter.*] That's an old trick . . . he must have pulled a doublecross on you, and then, to keep up appearances, they have pretended to capture him.

Isaac. [*Terrified.*] A spy? Has it come to that? A spy in my shop?

Reporter. They're called informers.

Isaac. [*Looking up at* Ariadne.] What will we do?

Ariadne. We can't do anything. We're besieged.

Isaac. [*To the* Reporter.] Did you hear? Besieged! [*Downcast.*] Oppression and violence again.

Reporter. [*Takes a step backward and tilts his head to see the typewriter better.*] It's my seventh.

Isaac. What?

Reporter. My seventh siege. Once in Casablanca, when I was young, then two in Algeria, one in China during an uprising against foreigners, and the last time in Guatemala, stuck for a week in the State Building because of a military coup.

Isaac. Then you've got some experience! Thank God! What do you think we should do?

Reporter. What all people under siege do—organize a defense. After the siege, there is usually an attack. By the way, do you have a telephone?

Isaac. [*Pointing to an old phone on the wall.*] Over there!

Reporter. [*He cranks the handle and puts the receiver to his ear.*] Hello . . . Hello . . . [*He hangs up.*] Just as I thought, they've cut the wires. Who knows when I'll be able to phone this story in to my newspaper?

[*In the meantime,* Ariadne, Moko, *and* Chanusky *have come down to the ground floor, while* Tanya, Chalcedony, *and* Cosmo *have come on stage from different directions. Heavy blows are heard from above.*]

Reporter. [*Looking up.*] What's that?

A Deep, Rhythmic Voice. The constituted authority orders you to surrender in the name of the Law.

Reporter. [*To* Isaac.] How should we answer?

Isaac. [*Confused.*] I don't know. You're the one who knows about these things.

Reporter. We'll try to talk . . . [*He cups his hands around his mouth and shouts up.*] Can you send someone to discuss terms?

Deep Voice. We don't discuss terms with rebels . . . You must surrender unconditionally.

Reporter. [*To* Isaac.] Do you hear that?

Isaac. But why are we rebels?

Reporter. [*Impatiently.*] That's a dumb question! Since the beginning of time, those who don't submit automatically become rebels.

Isaac. [*Quite irritated.*] I am tired of surrendering! I have been surrendering for thousands of years! I've had enough! I'm not taking any more orders. I'd rather die.

Reporter. [*Cupping his hands to his mouth, he shouts up.*] We refuse to surrender! [*Silence, then to* Isaac.] Do you have a flag we can run up?

Isaac. A flag? What for?

Reporter. Not for me, for you. If you don't have a flag, you are considered defectors, and if they capture you they can put you up against the wall.

Isaac. [*Huffily.*] This is all so complicated! [*To* Ariadne.] Do you have a flag?

Ariadne. Here's one! [*She goes to where the red jacket with the braid has been lying and ties the sleeves to a cord hanging from a pulley;* Moko *and* Chanusky *begin pulling on the rope and the jacket rises and catches a sudden wind that causes it to flutter. Everyone raises an arm as though saluting, and they shout: "Hurrah!"*]

The curtain closes quickly.

ACT 2

SCENE 1

Same scene as Act 1. In the dead of night. The warehouse is lit by old carriage lanterns placed here and there. Then, as the light of dawn appears and diffuses, the lanterns dim and finally go out.

As the curtain opens, downstage right, in the same place where Ariadne *was playing cards, there is an antiquated treadle sewing machine, from which a piece of blue cloth drapes to the ground: it forms a backdrop for a composition with the figures of* Ariadne *and* Cosmo, *who are seated on the ground and embracing in the pose of a classic statue. Still in the foreground, but downstage to the left, sitting on the large chest of furs, is the* Reporter *in shirt sleeves, with an unlit pipe between his teeth.*

In front of him, on a small table, are the typewriter and a bottle of brandy. The Reporter *is typing, stopping every once in a while to check what he has written on the sheet of paper; then he remains pensive and, if inspiration does not come to him, he takes a drink of liquor. On one of the transverse balconies, an actor made up like a mannequin (egg-shaped head and round joints) marches back and forth with wooden steps, carrying a stick at shoulder arms position. Every so often he stops, makes some movement from the manual of arms like an ancient Prussian sentinel, then begins to walk again. This business should take place during the longer pauses in the dialogue, so that it does not distract the audience.*

Reporter. [*Typing two or three words at a time while he reads aloud.*] A dusky night . . . a night of waiting and premonitions . . . like pale yellow sapphires forgotten by a fleeing thief, the lanterns glimmer among the stairs and balconies . . . The appointment with dawn is postponed to the year . . . [*He stops, remains pensive, then goes on.*] I write these hurried notes in a crypt that arose from the delirious calculations of an architect whose passion was cave exploring. I write without knowing when these lines will solidify into lead type, roll on the cylinders of the press, fly on wings of paper wet with ink . . . [Cosmo *pulls his lips away from* Ariadne's *and looks toward the rear of the stage where it is darker, as though he has heard a noise.* Ariadne *remains for an instant with her head thrown back, then she slowly recomposes herself, though she keeps her arms wrapped around the young man.*]

Ariadne. What is it?

Cosmo. Nothing, my dear . . .

Ariadne. You are always turning around as though someone is calling you.

Cosmo. [*Pensive.*] But no one is there. [*Kisses* Ariadne *again, as though to reassure her.*]

Reporter. [*Begins typing again.*] Above us is the steel spider of the besieging forces; it creeps with cruel slowness in preparation for the assault. A few yards away from me, in the spider web of the night, two entwined souls seek each other across the obstacle of their bodies. [*Pause, then he begins again.*] I see their quick glances . . . never a smile. Perhaps upon the lovers weighs the fragile reality of each precarious encounter. [*Stops again, takes a slug of brandy, and remains pensive.*]

Ariadne. [*Slides her face down into one of* Cosmo's *hands and nuzzles it.*] You smell like wheat.

Cosmo. [*With a quiet laugh.*] Wheat?

Ariadne. [*Looking at him tenderly.*] And warm bread.

Cosmo. I'm not sure what you smell like, but I drink you in as I used to breathe the fresh air when I came out of the mine.

Ariadne. [*After a pause.*] Tell me again about your hometown sprinkled with sulfur and about the volcano frosted with snow, and of the holidays that blossomed like carnations.

Cosmo. I no longer have a town, my love. I burned it along with my last cigarette, before I left.

Ariadne. You wanted to leave, to go to America so much?

Cosmo. I don't have America any more. I have only you and my screwdriver. [*Draws it from his belt like a dagger.*] To plunge into my heart when I can no longer bear living. [Ariadne *suddenly draws him to her, choking the words on his lips.*]

Reporter. [*Beginning to type again.*] Feverish words . . . and each kiss

is as unexpected as a slap. Then they are motionless, illuminated
by silence, sculptured by silence in the dark marble of the night.
[*Stops and remains pensive.*]

Ariadne. [*Slowly freeing herself.*] I still see you as I did the first day,
my love . . . and the smile you had that day. You looked at me
with your gentle, flashing eyes, and I knew joy and fear.

Cosmo. I, too, felt joy and fear. You looked like a queen, and if my
brother hadn't been there I would have kneeled.

Ariadne. [*With a sad smile.*] The queen of old rags . . .

Cosmo. I saw no rags . . . A hundred bells were ringing in my head,
a hundred stars sparkled in your hair. Then you began to sing
and your voice carried me away, as the wind does clouds, to the
heavens . . . [*Stops and turns toward the rear of the stage.*]

Ariadne. Again?

Cosmo. [*Rising.*] Didn't you hear it?

Ariadne. [*Rises unwillingly.*] It must be the mice. They are every-
where, but they don't bother anybody. [*Smiles.*] They are tame.
They will come and eat crumbs from the palm of your hand.
And they are warm and soft, with little pink feet.

Cosmo. [*Still leaning toward the rear.*] I didn't hear with my ears . . .

Ariadne. [*Squinting her eyes.*] I don't see anything.

Cosmo. [*A bit impatiently.*] Not with your eyes . . .

Reporter. [*Rising heavily.*] The boy is right.

Cosmo. [*Suddenly anxious.*] Do you think our isolation may be playing tricks on us?

Reporter. [*With his legs spread, wavering a little.*] Isolation is an
opinion . . .

Ariadne. I don't see and I don't hear anything. I want to see and
hear only you.

Cosmo. It has nothing to do with us.

Ariadne. [*Absentmindedly.*] With what, then?

Cosmo. [*Suddenly excited.*] Things that pass close to you, and you
can't touch them. Like somebody was watching you behind your
back . . . You turn around and nobody's there. [*Pointing into the
shadows.*] Don't you have a feeling somebody's coming closer?
[*Draws away, slightly frightened.*] There, it's gone now . . .

Ariadne. [*To the* Reporter.] But I don't feel anything . . . Why?
[*Bewildered and staring off into space.*] Don't I deserve anything?
[*As though to herself.*] Excluded from the mystery.

Reporter. [*Goes to replenish his courage from the bottle.*] You've got a
nice receiver but not for pulling in long distance broadcasts.
[*Sniggers.*] Only local ones, I would say . . . [*A scuffling occurs on*

the balcony where the mannequin armed with a stick is fighting, giving imaginary bayonet thrusts to the right and left with his wooden stick, as though defending himself from an invisible assailant.]

Cosmo. [*Pointing.*] Even the sentry is alarmed.

Ariadne. [*Speaking to herself.*] Even the mannequins, with their souls of straw . . . I am farther down, even lower than they are.

Reporter. [*Sitting down to his typewriter.*] Don't be scared. In every entrenched camp, at night, one's imagination runs wild . . . even becomes threatening. [*Taking the bottle.*] That's when you have to take it easy and not go off the deep end into the irrational. [*Drinks. Far away muffled shots are heard.*]

Ariadne. [*Startled.*] They are shooting!

Reporter. What did I just tell you? The sentries on the siege force are shooting at the silvery target of the moon.

Ariadne. But what if they have broken in somewhere?

Reporter. No one can have gotten into this fortress. I have had piles of plates and glasses put in all the passageways, and strings of bells on the curtains. Whoever tried to get in would cause pandemonium.

Cosmo. My brother's idea was better. With a barrier of electric wires, no one could get through.

Reporter. A great idea . . . if they hadn't shut off the current.

Cosmo. [*To himself.*] If they shut off the water, too, we are lost.

Ariadne. Don't worry, we have a cistern.

Reporter. [*Disgusted.*] Don't mention cisterns to me, for Christ's sake. That is the classic sanctuary for drowned people. [*Takes a drink of the brandy.*]

Ariadne. [*To* Cosmo.] You're trembling . . . Darling . . . get hold of yourself, calm down.

Cosmo. Do you think I am afraid? To die here or in the mine, it's the same thing. [*Smiling.*] But if I had died in the mine, I would never have known you.

Tanya. [*Appearing on the balcony in a nightgown and cap.*] Didn't you hear anything?

Reporter. Yes, madam, a false alarm.

Tanya. Shots and cries . . . Why don't they go ahead and attack? [*With her usual hallucinatory diction.*] Anything is better than this interminable waiting, even invasion and death!

Reporter. [*Impatient.*] Let's not joke about such things, madam. You don't know what a bayonet in your ribs is.

Tanya. [*Touching her breasts.*] Oh, yes . . . I can imagine it . . . the flash of a cold steel blade. [*Slight pause, then dreamily.*] A red geranium that blossoms on the breast . . . life gushing out in spurts . . . and the astonished soldier, uncertain whether he should strike a second blow . . . already frozen in the pose that he will have on his pedestal, and in his eyes the horror of the murderer who has been promoted to Hero. [*A pause, then in an affected voice.*] My dear sir, have you perchance seen my husband?

Reporter. [*Absentmindedly.*] I haven't seen him, madam.

Tanya. Can you at least tell me where he is standing guard?

Reporter. [*Consults a notebook.*] Well, let's take a look. The letter C . . . Candy stores . . . Capitals . . . Chambers of Commerce . . . Chambermaids . . . Chancellors . . . Chanusky . . . Here it is. Chanusky, from midnight to two in the morning, gallery of the two plaster statues . . . [*To* Tanya.] That must be that stretch of walkway that goes from the fork of the three wardrobes to the section with the bicycle parts.

Cosmo. It's my turn to relieve him. [*To* Tanya.] I'm sorry for being late.

Tanya. [*Condescendingly.*] Think nothing of it. Your youth excuses you.

Ariadne. [*To* Tanya.] As you know, I don't need any excuses.

Cosmo. [*Kissing* Ariadne *quickly on the hair.*] Good-bye, my love.

[*In two bounds he reaches the trap door and disappears with a swirl.*]

Tanya. [*Who in the meantime has come down to the first floor.*] Sir . . .

Reporter. Yes?

Tanya. How do you feel?

Reporter. Me? Quite well.

Tanya. [*Looking around her.*] I meant . . . do you feel lonely?

Reporter. That's a ridiculous question. We are always lonely and never alone.

Tanya. [*Like someone who is making a confession that has been held back a long time.*] I'm always surrounded by unknown forces, always beset by mysterious vibrations . . . Always derided by a network of memories . . .

Reporter. [*Beginning to drum nervously with his fingers on the table.*] Madam, please . . .

Tanya. [*Angrily.*] Don't blame my nerves, and especially not my imagination. [*As if to herself.*] The invisible presses us from every side, spies on us from every peephole, breathes from every crack. And all the while it is judging us. [*Looking around her, frightened.*] What if they are ghosts?

Reporter. [*Makes a discouraged gesture, then leafs through his notebook.*]

The letter G . . . Gallows . . . Gargoyle . . . Ghetto . . . No, there is no ghost. You can go sleep in peace now. I have marked down here everything we have on hand . . .

Tanya. Thank you, sir, thank you. Please excuse me. [*Leaves murmuring.*] There is no ghost . . . Thank God . . . There is no ghost!

Reporter. [*Rising and approaching* Ariadne *who has gone to sit down at the sewing machine, remaining pensive.*] What are you thinking about?

Ariadne. [*Gazing into space.*] It isn't important.

Reporter. Nothing is important, and everything is important.

Ariadne. I meant . . . nothing of interest . . .

Reporter. [*Completing the phrase.*] . . . to normal people, I agree. But I'm a drunkard, so I can understand you. [*Slight pause.*] The boy?

Ariadne. Oh, please . . .

Reporter. You are torn between the desire to hold onto him and the necessity of letting him go.

Ariadne. I have to let him go. His brother has turned all the money that they had over to that guy who is supposed to stow them away on board. They have burned their bridges behind them.

Reporter. And you are too much in love to accept that. Well, you are just the right age for suffering.

Ariadne. So long as *he* doesn't suffer . . . He treats me like a queen. If he only knew . . .

Reporter. [*As if to himself.*] Love is always a punishment for someone.

Ariadne. [*Almost crying.*] For me, only for me . . . [*Pause, then sadly.*] Even the thought of coming back down to earth makes my head spin . . . If only he wouldn't find out . . . if he can just continue his flight.

Reporter. [*Slightly moved, but trying not to show it.*] Come on, cheer up. Things may turn out all right. Why do you deny to destiny its privilege of springing one of its surprises?

Ariadne. Destiny is hard and cold.

Reporter. [*Good-naturedly.*] Oh, no . . . Sometimes it is also a magician. We expect one thing and presto! Out of his top hat he pulls colored ribbons and white rabbits.

Ariadne. [*Sighs.*] Let's hope so . . .

Reporter. I know so. You have to be optimistic. It has been a quiet night; everything is silent, and that is good for calming nerves. Why don't you go to bed?

[*A tremendous crash shakes the warehouse and cuts off his sentence. On the balcony, the mannequin collapses from fright and falls backward against the railing, his head and arms dangling. A muffled drum roll and far-off rumblings are heard, then stifled shouts.* Chanusky, Moko, *and* Tanya *crawl out from various places.*]

Tanya. [*Screaming.*] They are attacking! We are doomed! Peter, Peter, stay down!

Chanusky. [*To the* Reporter.] The artillery has opened fire. We've had it now!

Moko. Do you hear the tanks rumbling?

Tanya. [*Sniffing the air.*] I smell hydrogen and nitrogen.

Reporter. [*Excitedly.*] Cover your noses!

Tanya. It's no use, my whole body is experiencing a chain reaction.

Reporter. Be calm, be calm . . . Everyone to his battle station!

Chanusky. [*Desperate.*] But with what weapons, for God's sake?!

Reporter. [*To* Ariadne.] Where are the rifles that Isaac was talking about?

Ariadne. [*Trembling.*] They are old flintlock muskets. They are junk . . . They won't shoot.

Moko. What about those two sabers?

Ariadne. They are just painted wood.

Tanya. [*Indignant.*] The entire front is collapsing. No arms, no ammunition. We are at the mercy of the invader. And all because I wanted to be with Peter. Oh, how foolish I was!

Chalcedony. [*Appears on the sentinels' balcony and good-naturedly sets the puppet back on his feet.*] What is happening?

Tanya. [*Hysterically.*] Here is a man at last! You defend us; at least you have a screwdriver!

Chalcedony. [*Leans the mannequin, who has fallen down on him again, against the wall.*] Do you think I can defend you from thunder and hail? [*To the mannequin.*] Stand up, Roland! [*To the* Reporter *with slight irony.*] And you stand up, too, commander. It is only a thunderstorm.

Reporter. Well, I've been trying to calm them down. [*Wiping away the sweat and running to his bottle.*] Didn't you hear? [*He drinks.*] It's a thunderstorm, nothing but a storm.

Chalcedony. With rain and lightning. My brother told me; he made a reconnaissance patrol all the way up to the beginning of the walkway.

Reporter. [*To* Ariadne.] They'll even make me lose *my* head. And I served in the artillery! Imagine that!

Chanusky. [*Getting his breath back.*] If even the weather lays traps for us . . .

Moko. [*Grumbling.*] I'll remember that boom of the bass drum . . .

Chalcedony. [*Laughing.*] Go to sleep . . . Good night everybody. [*Exits.*]

[Tanya *reluctantly follows him, grumbling. The drumming of the hail gradually diminishes. A few rolls of thunder are still heard in the distance.*]

Chanusky. [*To the* Reporter.] Excuse me . . .

Reporter. Now what?

Tanya. [*Suddenly reappearing on the balcony.*] Peter, don't trust the fourth estate! [*Exits.*]

Chanusky. [*With a gesture of discouragement.*] Tanya, for God's sake . . . [*To the* Reporter.] You must excuse her. She has a noble soul, but full of complexes . . . and she really does love me.

Reporter. [*Visibly annoyed.*] She's excused. Now what do you want to talk to me about?

Chanusky. The prize . . .

Reporter. [*Snorting.*] That again? I've already promised you that I'll look into it . . . As soon as I am free, of course. [*Patiently.*] I'll go to the Bureau of Awards and Prizes—the undersecretary is an old friend of mine; we flunked the same exams—and I'll ask him to take charge of the whole affair. [*Changing tone.*] By the way, do you already have your request?

Chanusky. What request?

Reporter. A request neatly typed on legal-sized paper . . . bureaucrats have a weakness for legal paper . . . "I, the undersigned Peter Chanusky, a man without a country residing nowhere, respectfully request et cetera, et cetera . . ." In short, you can't expect to receive a prize without a dossier, a document ornamented with notary seals, signatures, caveats, and subclauses . . . And only after we have exhausted all the normal channels will we turn to the press, we'll mount a scandalmongering campaign. [*Emphatically.*] "Man waits twenty years for prize" . . . and for a subtitle . . . "an injustice that must be corrected, et cetera, et cetera . . ." Okay?

Chanusky. But I don't want the prize any more.

Reporter. [*Bewildered.*] You don't want the prize any more?

Chanusky. No, I have decided to refuse it.

Reporter. [*Raising his arms.*] I just don't understand you. You are incoherence personified. Ever since I set foot in this cave, you and your wife have done nothing but plead . . . one for the prize, the other for an appointment to the Ladies' Auxiliary. Did I dream it? I even told you that I would have my political friends look into the matter . . . I've got friends in every party, since I have had to change my politics whenever my newspaper changed publishers.

Chanusky. That's very true, and I am here to thank you sincerely, even on my wife's behalf, for everything you were willing to do for us. But what can I say? We have changed our minds, that's all.

Reporter. Your wife, too? And when did you change your minds?

Chanusky. [*After a moment's hesitation.*] Tonight . . . [*Looks for words while* Ariadne *stops sewing and listens.*] In a dream . . . Actually we weren't sleeping . . . How can I explain it? We were in that state of lucid daze that overcomes sentinels when they fight sleep . . . [*Slight pause.*] Too tired to talk or even to think, we were still clearheaded. [*As though talking to himself.*] The soul tied to a string, like a balloon about to escape from a child's hand; and you hold your breath . . . your gaze fixed on a single geometrical point, consciousness paralyzed in nothingness.

Reporter. [*Grabbing a notebook.*] Wait, let me get this down.

Chanusky. [*As though speaking to himself.*] How long were we in that almost suspended state? A minute or a century? I have no idea. At a certain moment, a voice speaks out but it comes from no one direction, a voice unheard by ears, a voice that was at the same time inside and outside of us; all it said was: "Goest thou, without the help of anything, throughout the land."

Reporter. [*Taking notes.*] "Thou?" . . . in the singular?

Chanusky. Yes, but each of us had heard it, so the result was really plural. [*Slight pause.*] Then we realized that our lives, which up to that point had been weighed down with unsatisfied desires, vile grudges, absurd hopes, and obscure instincts, had suddenly become simplified, like a cloud-covered sky swept clean by a fresh breeze from the glaciers.

Ariadne. [*Listening intently.*] Then what?

Chanusky. [*Exhausted.*] That's all.

Reporter. What do you mean, "that's all"? What were your reactions? What did you say to each other?

Chanusky. There was nothing to say. We had been absolved, we were free.

Ariadne. [*Like an echo.*] Absolved . . . free.

Reporter. Okay. [*Holds out the notebook and pen to* Chanusky.] Would you mind authenticating this interview with your signature? The newspaper might want to run a photograph of it.

Chanusky. [*Drawing back.*] Actually, I didn't intend to give an interview . . . [*With an indignant gesture he pushes the notebook away.*]

How can you think that I could agree to compromises of this
sort?

Reporter. [*Shrugging his shoulders.*] I'm just doing my job.

Chanusky. You are the most cynical person I have ever met . . . You
want to profit from the supernatural, play up the miracle for
commercial purposes, solidify in mute gray linotype characters
nuances that are scarcely perceptible, conversations that the
soul hardly dares to murmur in the pale light of dusk.

Reporter. [*Snorting.*] How the editors evaluate my article and what
they make of it in print have nothing to do with me.

Ariadne. Why spoil his joy at being absolved, at being free?

Reporter. [*Angrily.*] I'm not spoiling anything! My job is to write
articles. Then the historians will come along and twist everything around.

Chanusky. You are arrogant, too.

Reporter. [*After plucking up his courage with a drink of brandy.*] Now
you listen to me. If there had been newspapers two thousand
years ago and if today we had a copy of the *Bethlehem Gazette*
dated December 25th, you would only have to glance at the
birth announcements to put an end to all the polemics of those
respected historians.

Ariadne. [*To the* Reporter *with sudden anxiety.*] Something is going to
happen. I can feel it in my bones, poor devil that I am; and I
don't expect miracles that certainly I don't deserve, but something is going to happen, it's going to happen.

Reporter. [*Getting up and lighting his pipe.*] Something can always
happen. We are living in times when the cosmos creaks and
maybe the universe is about to crumble. That's one more reason
to keep a tight rein on our emotions.

Moko. [*Appearing from the rear staircase.*] Don't you think that everyone's been talking for too long about this Apocalypse? What if it
was just a trick dreamed up by arms merchants?

Reporter. [*Squinting.*] Oh, it's you. It's not easy to see you in the
dark . . . But aren't you supposed to be on guard duty? [*Goes to
consult the notebook.*] At post number five?

Moko. I just came to tell you that I am not going to take any more
turns at guard duty. In fact, I want to resign from being a
soldier.

Reporter. Now what? Are we going to have conscientious objectors,
too?

Moko. I'm not objecting. I've changed my mind.

Reporter. A deviationist, then? Or still worse, a dissident?

Moko. Don't condemn me before you have heard me out. There has been a change in me. I don't want to be involved in any acts of violence in this war, especially since, among other things, I don't know what caused it.

Chanusky. [*Conciliatory.*] Did anyone ever know exactly why wars break out?

Moko. Maybe the men in power know, and the military leaders, too . . .

Reporter. They think they know, they say they know . . . Then they write their memoirs to show that their good faith was taken unawares, that they were political innocents allergic to war.

Moko. Well, anyway, I've told you how I feel about it.

Reporter. I must point out to you that your jacket was run up as the flag of our resistance.

Moko. My jacket? Oh, no. that was a lion-tamer's jacket. I'm a musician. I live in a two-dimensional world—tempo and rhythm.

Reporter. Listen, I don't want to get involved in your crises of conscience, but if you want to be white . . .

Moko. [*Angrily.*] No, no! I don't want to be white any more!

Reporter. Ah, so that's it. [*Turning slightly to the others.*] You have decided to drive me crazy. [*Grabs the bottle and, speaking to himself.*] Come on, get hold of yourself, get hold of yourself. [*He drinks.*]

Moko. Now, don't take it so hard . . . Tonight I couldn't get to sleep . . .

Reporter. But you had a canopied bed from the fifteenth century!

Moko. I felt faint, nauseated . . . At first I thought a fever was coming on. My heart was beating against my rib cage, my temples throbbed, if I closed my eyes I saw flashes. Finally, I let out a deep sigh, or rather . . . *I* didn't . . . I *heard* a deep sigh, and then I had a sensation of freedom, and as though someone else had prompted me, I exclaimed out loud: "I was born black and black I want to stay!"

Reporter. Even if you don't know Africa?

Moko. Maybe Africa knows me . . . it is seeking me. Maybe that sigh came from far away, from the equatorial forests that my ancestors were dragged from to become slaves.

Reporter. [*Nervously.*] Primitive echoes . . . ancestral superstitions . . . the eternal return of magic tribal rituals. You are the victim of the totemic unconscious, of the original clan!

Moko. [*Humbly.*] You could be right, sir. But I have told you truthfully what happened to me.

Chanusky. [*As though absorbed.*] Something similar happened to me, too . . . Maybe we have entered into a spiritual zone of our existence.

Reporter. [*Angrily.*] We've got to keep our feet on the ground! We have to correct misleading appearances . . . adjust our inhibitory centers. [*He drinks.*]

Isaac. [*Appearing from the rear.*] You are at war with yourself, my dear sir. You are besieged by your own incredulity and, to quote the prophet Jeremiah, you have ears and you hear not, you have eyes and see not.

Reporter. [*To* Isaac.] Now you aren't going to tell me that you have changed, too, at your age? [Isaac, *instead of answering, goes to a gong and strikes three blows that echo sonorously beneath the vaults. Emerging from passageways, scampering down rope ladders, climbing over furniture and draperies,* Tanya, Chalcedony, *and* Cosmo *appear.*]

Reporter. [*Surprised.*] The signal to assembly? You've gone crazy!

Isaac. I have important news to announce.

Reporter. News that I, a newsman, know nothing about? [*To* Chanusky.] I'm afraid that everybody around here has gone off his rocker.

Isaac. [*Solemnly raising his arms.*] The great day has come . . . Those who live on the outside have certainly already noticed the signs that accompany the fulfillment of the ages. They have seen bats fly like eagles, the wolf lie down with the lamb, the ant emerge unharmed from beneath the hoof of the elephant. On your knees! . . . for the long waiting has come to an end, and the Chosen One has descended among us. [Ariadne *and* Cosmo *are the only ones who fall to their knees while the others remain dumbfounded.*]

Reporter. [*Angrily.*] Would you please tell me what this oration is all about?

Isaac. [*In a sad but slightly ironic voice.*] How can a mere thinking machine understand? Oh, I know . . . Did you think it was mice scratching, water gurgling in the pipes, wind blowing in the corridors? No, my dear sir, I was born in this den, and I know its every palpitation, every sigh, every lament. If I say that the Lord has arrived, you can believe it.

Reporter. [*Amazed.*] The Lord?

Isaac. The Lord of the living and the dead . . . he who will reward the just and punish the evil, he who will lift up the humble and render justice to the innocent, console the afflicted and proclaim on Earth the reign of God!

Reporter. [*Jumps up.*] Damn! [*He streaks for the telephone, but his hand drops as it almost reaches the receiver.*] Oh, hell! I forgot they cut the line.

Isaac. Who do you want to call?

Reporter. You don't know? Why, if what you say is true, I've got to let my newspaper know. [*Excitedly.*] Do you realize what an exclusive piece of news like this means? There will be a full-page headline and at least four or five extra editions. [*Running to the typewriter.*] In the meantime I'd better knock out a first draft. [*Rips the sheet from the platen, puts in another and begins to type.*] The cathedral of rags has its God! [*Nervously.*] No, no, it needs something stronger! [*Cancels what he has written with a line of x's.*] The great promise has been kept! [*Cancels it out.*] That's no good, either! Too general! It has to be a breathtaking title. [*To* Isaac.] By the way, why do you think that He should choose to come here?

Isaac. Where should he go except among the besieged? Not to help us, of course. [*Slight pause.*] Perhaps just to observe us. [*Sniggers.*] Microbes in a test tube, examined by the great lens of his dark eye.

Reporter. [*Striking his fist on the table.*] That's great! There's the title! The eye of God in the fortress of rags! [*After having typed out the title.*] And now for the details . . . [*To* Isaac.] Okay . . . What was the exact time of arrival? What sensations did you experience? What were the first words that you exchanged with the Divinity?

Isaac. [*Indignantly.*] Why, you are blaspheming, sir!

Reporter. [*Snorting.*] Here we go again! First he announces earth-shaking news, and then he refuses to give us the details. [*Takes a drink of brandy.*] I'll try to help you . . . A minute ago you told me that the Lord had come here to observe us. But earlier you were talking about punishments.

Isaac. Certainly. The Lord must punish us. [*Slight pause.*] And all the while he will weep.

Reporter. [*Typing.*] And all the while he will weep . . . [*Stupefied by what he has written.*] What do you mean, he will weep?

Isaac. [*Losing patience.*] He's already weeping . . . Don't you hear him? Ah, I understand, you are thinking of human lamentations, of the grotesque weeping of men. But this is completely different, sir, completely different!

Reporter. [*Typing.*] The principal witness declares that he has heard suprahuman weeping . . . [*Getting up nervously.*] No, we won't get anywhere like this. I need facts, tangible facts, you understand. I can't go chasing after somebody who has heard a voice, another who sleepwalks, you who hear celestial weeping . . .

Isaac. [*Angrily.*] Who do you think you are?! You should fall on your knees first! [*Turning to the others.*] You should all fall on your knees and and confess your guilt.

Tanya. [*Kneeling.*] I am ready! On the 14th of April 1940 when I was still a naive young girl and I was vacationing with my family on the beach at Santa Marinella, I could not resist watching a bearded man who was making obscene gestures.

Reporter. [*Interrupting her.*] For God's sake, lady, nobody asked you for anything like that. [*To* Isaac.] Listen . . . I accepted the war because I'm getting used to their bad habit of breaking out without any warning. I accepted the siege because of fortuitous circumstances. You must admit that to atone for the acquisition of a secondhand typewriter with a subterranean adventure that will last we don't know how long presupposes on the part of the purchaser an enormous amount of tolerance. Now, must I also accept—without the slightest proof—a piece of news that would change the entire course of history?

Isaac. [*Shrugging his shoulders.*] The Lord is accessible only via a personal path. Every human being has his life and his God.

Reporter. But I have a responsibility to my readers! And what about the competition from other newspapers? Naturally, no one knows better than I do how to put across a news story, and that is why I took notes on everything that has happened that was even a little out of the ordinary: dreams, visions, mysterious voices. They will be useful in writing what we journalists call the lead. But those are just words that the reader skims through rapidly in order to get to the meat of the story, the blockbuster. [*Slight pause.*] And it has to be something that will make a splash, a big splash . . . Where is it? I don't see it, I don't hear it.

[*At that moment there is a crash of pottery and breaking glass as well as a long ringing of bells. Those who were kneeling jump to their feet, and everyone looks up toward the highest part of the warehouse.*]

Chanusky. [*Frightened.*] We've had it! Someone has got in by the northeast corridor!

Tanya. It's the invasion! . . . Help!

[*At the top of the central stairway appear two mannequins holding the arms of a short, stocky fellow, with a bowler hat. He is wearing a cashmere coat and checkered pants.*]

Isaac. [*Lifting his arms.*] Ah! The man who wanted the beaver collar!

Moko. [*Stupefied.*] The little guy with the checkered pants!

Reporter. The secret agent has fallen into the trap!

Ariadne. [*To* Isaac.] What did I tell you? When a customer gets a hankering after an object, he always comes back.

[*The prisoner manages to free himself and runs down the stairs while the two mannequins stay at the top, their legs spread wide, in the military rest position. The newcomer is a chubby little man, with his moustache curled in a romantic way, and who speaks and moves with ease; but beneath his apparent good humor, there is in him something cunning and clever.*]

The Little Man. I am Mr. Brandolisio, a dealer in fancy hides and skins, and I protest this outrageous detention.

Isaac. [*Crosses his arms.*] Do you recognize me?

Brandolisio. [*Without even looking at him.*] No, sir.

Moko. Are you saying that we did not meet last week in the walkways of this warehouse, and to be more precise, in the corridor near the cistern?

Tanya. [*Raising her arms to heaven.*] God have mercy! Poison! Pollution of our drinking water!

Brandolisio. [*Without looking at* Moko.] I don't know what cistern you are talking about.

Ariadne. Don't you even remember having asked for a beaver collar?

Brandolisio. At the risk of being discourteous, I must say no. Anyway, I'm a married man with a family.

Reporter. Well, would you please explain how you got in here?

Brandolisio. Without admitting the legitimacy of your question, I can nonetheless easily answer it. I was just passing by. I slipped in a puddle—it rained a lot tonight—I tried to grab onto the doorpost of the entrance but I lost my footing and ended up in a pile of plates. Then these two armed men came along. [*Approaches* Tanya.] Excuse me, madam, do you have a mirror?

Tanya. [*Taking a mirror from her purse.*] Here you are! [*Holds it up to* Brandolisio *who carefully adjusts his necktie.*]

Brandolisio. Thank you. [*Returns to where he was.*] I have nothing more to add. I beg to be returned to my family and to my business associates.

Reporter. Not before you tell us what approaches, understandings, and contacts you have had with the intelligence service of the besieging forces.

Brandolisio. I really do not know what intelligence service you are referring to and by what right you are subjecting me to interrogation.

Reporter. [*With a shaking voice and pointing his finger at* Brandolisio.] You are a spy and you will be tried for high treason.

Brandolisio. [*Coming to attention and clicking his heels.*] Very well, sir, but since I am a second lieutenant in the territorial militia reserves, I request to be placed under house arrest and not subjected to the humiliation of incarceration.

Reporter. Request granted. Are you armed?

Brandolisio. [*Taking a penknife from his pocket and handing it to him.*] A penknife for advertising purposes . . . It even carries the name of my company.

Isaac. [*Triumphantly to the* Reporter.] You asked for proof? Here is the proof. [*Falls to his knees.*] Lord, I thank you! [*All kneel, while an astounded* Mr. Brandolisio *takes off his hat.*]

Brandolisio. [*Murmuring.*] Please . . . Please . . . This really isn't necessary . . . Please . . .

The stage darkens.

SCENE 2

A few days or weeks or years have passed. The setting is the same but without the sewing machine. From above, the reddish light of a setting sun filters through; it will gradually intensify toward the end of the scene. All the characters are present; some like Chalcedony *and* Moko *are squatting on the floor with their backs leaning against furniture or a wall; others, like* Cosmo *and* Chanusky, *are standing with their hands in their pockets.* Isaac *is sitting in an old armchair with a Bible in his hands. The* Reporter, *his elbows resting on the typing table, is contemplating the empty bottle.* Tanya *strolls about waving a lace fan, and* Ariadne *is squatting on a stool. Sitting off by himself, with his legs crossed and a fat cigar in his mouth,* Mr. Brandolisio *is smoking in little puffs. At first sight, the characters will seem more numerous because of the presence of mannequins—real ones this time—scattered among the actors, with their same tired poses and their eyeless faces staring off into emptiness. A layer of dust on the clothing will give the impression that much time has passed. When the curtain rises, all is motionless and silent.*

Reporter. [*With a sigh.*] No more bottles, no more inspiration. This is one of the consequences of the siege that I had not foreseen.

Tanya. [*In an affected tone of voice.*] Does your typewriter not suggest to you some amusement that will help us pass the time? A nice parlor game perhaps?

Chanusky. [*Discouraged.*] Tanya, how can you think of parlor games?

Tanya. I just said that to have something to say. Don't always take me so literally. [*To the* Reporter.] Could you tell us some picturesque adventure—truth or fiction, it doesn't matter—about your life as a roving reporter?

Reporter. [*Rising*] The lady's wishes are the gentleman's command. [*After a moment of gathering his thoughts.*] I'll tell you an unusual adventure I had one summer when I was doing a feature entitled "Strange Itineraries." One evening, after a rather tiring trip on muleback, I found myself in Lutarca . . .

Brandolisio. Where is Lutarca?

Reporter. Now don't start interrupting . . . Lutarca is in the upper Gerbasina valley, which takes its name from the Gerba river. Julius Caesar mentions it in his *De bello gallico.*

Brandolisio. At that time it was called Lutreca.

Reporter. [*Visibly irritated.*] Okay, it was called Lutreca.

Brandolisio. And it wasn't Caesar who mentioned it, but Strabo in his polemic with Eratosthenes . . .

Reporter. [*Angrily.*] Oh, my God! Well, you tell it then . . . Tell us all about modern Lutarca and ancient Lutreca.

Brandolisio. [*Flicking his cigar ash.*] It doesn't seem to me a very interesting subject.

Reporter. [*His voice trembling.*] Mr. Brandolisio, this is not the first time that you have sabotaged my projects.

Tanya. [*To the* Reporter.] You could be more courteous to a guest.

Reporter. [*Irritated.*] What do you mean, a "guest"! Mr. Brandolisio is a prisoner, and moreover he has been condemned to be shot!

Tanya. A sentence that we can't carry out because we have no firearms.

Reporter. Anyway, I was speaking of Lutarca as I would speak of any other poetic subject of discourse.

Brandolisio. [*Placidly.*] Would you recite poetry to convicts?

Reporter. Why not? Poetry is the individual's attempt to find what is true for everyone. Besides, we were just trying to pass the time.

Brandolisio. I think that in order to interest convicts, you would have to talk about freedom. Maybe read them a book on famous escapes.

Reporter. [*Ironically.*] . . . and talk to men about money and about love to women. [*Scornfully.*] You certainly are not overendowed with imagination, Mr. Brandolisio.

Ariadne. [*Tiredly.*] Mr. Brandolisio is right. After so many weeks of siege, don't you think that we are used to watching time pass? I'm not even aware of it any more.

Brandolisio. [*Looking off into space.*] And do you know why? Because time isn't passing any more. It has stopped . . . besieged along with us. Or rather, we are besieged by time, like the housefly in the freight car; it can fly all it wants, but it is still part of the train, and it is forced to travel at the same speed.

Reporter. [*Ironically.*] You almost seem to be insinuating that the siege has paralyzed our lives.

Brandolisio. I don't say that it has paralyzed our lives; I say that it has excluded tomorrow. We are always today, and we are almost unaware of the succession of days and nights . . .

Chanusky. How true that is! Bravo, Mr. Brandolisio! The siege has shattered a trajectory.

Brandolisio. Exactly.

Reporter. [*Scoffingly.*] Wait and see. The next thing, we'll have become immortal.

Brandolisio. In a certain sense, yes. At least as long as the siege lasts.

Moko. [*With a sigh.*] Without even knowing who is besieging us.

Brandolisio. What does it matter? Today all uniforms are alike. There are no soldiers any more, only robots, with earth-colored coveralls spotted with dirty green and faded orange . . . a helmet on their heads, a machine gun under their arms. It is hard to tell what nation they belong to, or if they are special police squads or the regular army.

Tanya. You are such a fascinating conversationalist, Mr. Brandolisio.

Brandolisio. Thank you, madam. When we get out, I would be honored to introduce you to my wife.

Tanya. [*While the* Reporter *snorts and makes gestures of intolerance.*] The honor will be mine, Mr. Brandolisio. Does your wife help you in your hide business?

Brandolisio. Actually, she used to help me. But since she has become the president of the International Association of Ladies' Auxiliaries, she has had very little time to devote to the business.

Tanya. [*With a little cry.*] Oh, what a strange coincidence! Just think! I, too, at a certain moment in my life . . .

Chanusky. [*Interrupting her.*] Tanya!

Tanya. [*Mortified.*] Oh, I'm sorry, Peter.

Brandolisio. Why, what's wrong? [*To Chanusky.*] Perhaps your wife once had noble aspirations that the contingencies of life prevented her from realizing.

Tanya. One can see that you understand women, Mr. Brandolisio.

Brandolisio. We were talking about my wife who is always burdened with a thousand obligations. Local publicity, international relations, cultural exchanges . . . And then there are the elections of Ladies' Auxiliary inspectors, who in turn choose the supervisors upon whom depends the recruitment of first-, second-, and third-class Lady Auxiliaries.

Tanya. [*Amazed.*] What marvelous organization!

Brandolisio. But would you believe it? Sometimes she is obliged to choose as first-class Lady Auxiliaries, first class, I say . . . women of modest extraction and of dubious culture.

Tanya. [*Stupefied.*] But how can that be, Mr. Brandolisio? I don't understand.

Brandolisio. A lack of candidates. We live in a century of youth . . . which is excellent, perhaps, from a certain viewpoint, but it is absolutely unsuitable for the heavy responsibilities that the role of Lady Auxiliary incurs.

Tanya. [*Stiffly, gravely.*] I think that, above all, it is also a question of style.

Brandolisio. Exactly . . . In a certain sense, you have to be born a Lady Auxiliary.

Tanya. [*Excitedly.*] Did you hear, Peter? You have to be born a Lady Auxiliary.

Brandolisio. The same thing happens in the D.P.N.P. Foundation.

Reporter. [*Increasingly sarcastic.*] I never heard of it.

Brandolisio. [*Impassively.*] That's strange. It received a lot of coverage in the press. [*Solemnly.*] D.P.N.P.—Distribution of Prizes to Neglected Passersby.

Chanusky. What? . . . What?

Brandolisio. It was funded by a donation from a benefactor, who also wished to remain unknown, in order to award annually a prize to someone who had never received one. It seems easy, doesn't it? But if you knew how hard it is . . . It is almost impossible to find someone who has never received an award or a prize or a certificate.

Chanusky. [*Laughing, somewhat embarrassed.*] Oh, that's it . . .

Brandolisio. Almost impossible, I tell you. It is so true that as president of the D.P.N.P. I am forced, every year, to postpone the award.

Chanusky. Then the prize must have doubled, tripled . . .

Brandolisio. It has multiplied thirty times. [*Flashes his fingers three times.*] Thirty . . . Plus the interest.

Chanusky. And you do not know who to give such an enormous prize to?

Brandolisio. First of all, I have to find an unknown passerby. An almost impossible task . . . Everyone nowadays is known, even renowned, with documents, addresses, telephones, television appearances, political awards, et cetera.

Chanusky. [*Shouting.*] Not me, Mr. Brandolisio, not me!

Brandolisio. Is it possible?

Chanusky. I do not know where I was born . . . my name is temporary . . . the year of my birth doubtful . . . Everything is uncertain, hypothetical, questionable. [*Decisively.*] Mr. Brandolisio, no passerby can be more unknown than I!

Brandolisio. [*To the* Reporter *with slight irony.*] Perhaps I have found some subjects that interest the besieged, even if I don't have a thinking typewriter. [*The* Reporter *scornfully turns his back to him.*]

Isaac. [*Lifting his eyes from the* Bible.] I warn you, Mr. Brandolisio, that in this place besieged by unknown persons, there have occurred certain events of a universal importance that have totally changed the mentality and the aspirations of everyone.

Brandolisio. I do not doubt that, Isaac, I do not doubt it. But it never hurts to test facts. Anyway, I only wanted to chat awhile, unpretentiously. [*Turning to the others.*] If these good people, to kill time, prefer to count to a hundred as insomniacs do, I certainly shall not disturb their counting.

Moko. [*With a sigh.*] Last night I counted to 2,000,753 and I still couldn't fall asleep.

Brandolisio. Why not?

Moko. Ehh . . . It would take a faucet to shut off the dripping of my thoughts. If a person could at a certain point turn a little handle . . . and click . . .

Brandolisio. Yes . . . There are so many useless inventions. [*Going toward* Chalcedony.] And how do you kill time while waiting to board ship?

Chalcedony. What can I do? I'm not educated. I went down into the mine when I was twelve years old, with the job of carrying water jugs into the galleries. Behind me walked the burro with the barrels. You know those little burros that always stay down in the mines? They've even got their stables down there, and their eyes are as blind as moles' eyes? Well . . . When the tunnel became so low that the burro couldn't go any further, I would fill the jug and crawling on my stomach I would carry it to the miner. I earned seven pennies a day.

Brandolisio. And you felt like you were already a man.

Chalcedony. I *was* a man. I took those seven pennies home, so I had the right to swear if my mother didn't put enough salt in the soup. Sundays, I would go to the tavern with my father, and I would talk with his buddies, all old folks.

Cosmo. Why don't you tell him what the watchmaker said? [*To* Brandolisio.] A smart man, you know, who read all kinds of books and even knew the stars. Some summer nights, he would point his finger up in the air and say the names of the stars. [*Smiling incredulously.*] Can stars actually have names like men do?

Chalcedony. [*Smiling at the memory.*] Sebastian Linguitti his name was, he was forty-eight, a watchmaker. He used to drink. Boy, could he drink . . . And when he was drunk enough, he would speak in proverbs.

Brandolisio. Proverbs?

Chalcedony. Yeah, in proverbs. I remember one that really stuck with me when I was a boy. He would say . . . the world is an ancient catastrophe.

Brandolisio. [*Thoughtfully.*] That's it . . . The world is an ancient catastrophe . . . Poor old Linguitti!

Chalcedony. [*Somewhat amazed.*] Did you know him?

Brandolisio. Sure . . . He died December 2, 1956, of cirrhosis of the liver.

Chalcedony. [*To* Cosmo.] Did you hear that?

Cosmo. [*Laughing, to* Brandolisio.] And the town doctor said he died of an ingrown toenail . . . What a dumbass!

Brandolisio. No, no . . . it was cirrhosis of the liver. [*Turning toward* Moko.] And what will you do after the siege ends?

Moko. Well, I'll go back to the Crazy Bat, a nightclub.

Brandolisio. A second-class one . . . Number 22 Museum Street, just beyond the newsstand.

Moko. [*Somewhat amazed.*] Have you been there?

Brandolisio. A few times . . . The owner was a heavyset fellow, with a strawberry birthmark near his nose.

Moko. Was? He is . . .

Brandolisio. Unfortunately, he is no longer. It was an autointoxication case.

Moko. He was driving drunk? He was hit by a drunk driver?

Brandolisio. No, no. Blood poisoning. He'd always had trouble with his blood.

Moko. Oh, I see . . . I'm sorry, I'm really sorry . . . He was a character! When a customer wasn't pleased with the service, he'd yell: "Go to the devil!" Then he'd laugh and say . . . "We'll be in hell together." [*Slight pause.*] As if he was sure he'd be going there, too.

Brandolisio. [*Breaks out in a dry little laugh halfway between a goat's bleating and the screech of a rusty chain.* Moko *stops as though frozen and, troubled by a vague uneasiness, looks at* Brandolisio. *Everyone turns to look at the little man who, having stopped laughing, has resumed his good-humored air.*] So you were saying that you would go back to the "Bat" . . .

Moko. To play the drums. If you used to go there, you ought to remember me.

Brandolisio. Certainly. You were the third from the left in the second row of the red-jacketed orchestra. Only you were always in shirt sleeves.

Moko. I wasn't a regular player then, but I have a contract now, and if, as I hope, the musicians' union has called a strike, I'll even get a pay raise.

Brandolisio. And what will you do with the money?

Moko. What money?

Brandolisio. What you will earn when you begin playing again.

Moko. [*Hostilely, sorrowfully.*] Ah, I don't know . . . I really don't know . . . Before, all my earnings ended up in the pockets of doctors, but at least I had an aim in life: I wanted to be white.

Isaac. [*Getting up and going toward* Brandolisio.] You know what? I have never been as sorry as I am today not to have a nice collection of automatic rifles.

Brandolisio. [*With a sigh.*] And yet you're probably a pacifist.

Isaac. [*Angrily.*] True, but your kind, who leads people into temptation, really deserves to be shot—or at the very least, hanged.

Brandolisio. Well, you have plenty of rope in your warehouse. But let's see if everybody thinks like you do.

Reporter. [*Picking up a rope from somewhere and making a hangman's noose.*] You certainly don't.

Brandolisio. [*To* Tanya.] And you, madam, would you hang me?

Tanya. Good heavens no, sir . . . Besides, I can't bear to see people with their tongues hanging out.

Brandolisio. [*To* Chanusky.] And you?

Chanusky. In principle, I am against violence.

Brandolisio. [*To* Chalcedony *and* Cosmo.] Are you anxious to hang me?

Chalcedony. That's not my job.

Cosmo. [*Smiling.*] Well, it certainly isn't mine . . . I'm just an apprentice.

Moko. [*To the* Reporter.] Put away that rope. With my vote, Mr. Brandolisio already has a majority.

Brandolisio. [*Giving a light caress to* Ariadne.] Even if this lovely young girl were against me . . . [*To* Moko.] But there is still time to think about it. And who knows? Maybe in the end I'll have all of you on my side.

Reporter. [*Throwing down the noose.*] Don't get your hopes up.

Isaac. As far as I'm concerned, you can get that idea out of your head.

Chanusky. [*To* Brandolisio.] And to think that they all used to like you!

[Brandolisio *breaks out again in his icy little laugh and a tremor passes across the faces of the characters.*]

Chanusky. [*After clearing his throat to pluck up his courage.*] Would you mind explaining to me how that thing works, that abbreviation?

Brandolisio. [*Good-natured again.*] The D.P.N.P.? It's very simple. Every day I stop a passerby at random, and I ask him: Who are you? What's your name? Do you know who you are? et cetera. The answers are almost always the same: I am So-and-So, here is my business card, my identification card, passport, driver's license, marriage certificate, high school diploma, et cetera. An awful lot of them have a cousin who is a judge and an archbishop for an uncle. Then I ask them: Have you ever received a prize? Sure, a good conduct medal or a first prize for silkworm growing, or who knows, an honorable mention from the S.P.C.A. [*In an amused tone.*] Then there are those who have received a prolific father award, a twenty-five-year service pin, a certificate for having given blood. In short, I end up thanking them, begging their pardon, and moving on.

Chanusky. Do you interview only one a day?

Brandolisio. One a day . . . 365 per year . . . 366 in leap years. That's quite a few, don't you think?

Tanya. [*Fanning* Brandolisio *with her fan.*] For someone like you, sir, even one a day is a lot, with all the other things you have to do.

Brandolisio. Indeed, I am involved in many things. [*Courteously moving the fan aside.*] Please, I don't like drafts . . . [*going toward* Chalcedony.] By the way, I forgot to ask you if you would be willing to work in a furnace factory.

Chalcedony. No, sir . . . You must forgive me, but I made a holy vow on the memory of my mother's soul. I swore that if I ever got out of the mine, I would never again work under anyone, not even my best friend. I'd rather starve all by myself.

Brandolisio. [*To* Cosmo.] What about you?

Cosmo. I do what my brother says.

Brandolisio. [*After studying the boy for a moment.*] And yet, I feel that we'll meet again soon . . . [*Turning to* Ariadne.] And you, sweet thing, what will you do in here?

Ariadne. [*Shrugging her shoulders.*] I'm the salesgirl. I mend rags, repair broken pottery, and show customers out.

Brandolisio. [*Thoughtful.*] Too bad I didn't think of that earlier. I've just lost a department head at Store Fifty-One. She was a good girl, but she married a prince, and . . . bye-bye.

Ariadne. [*Enchanted.*] A prince?

Brandolisio. It wasn't what you would call a marriage of love. Rather, it was an act of charity. The prince was bankrupt, but my department head, between her savings account, house, and car, saved that poor young man.

Isaac. [*Angrily.*] Mr. Brandolisio, there is no limit to your impudence. Are you trying to steal my salesgirl, too?

Reporter. [*Scornfully.*] Let him talk. I'm having a world of fun.

Ariadne. [*To* Isaac.] Maybe I'm your employee, but I'm not your slave, and I have the right to think about my future. [*To* Brandolisio.] He has never given me a regular salary . . . just a few old rags to cover me.

Brandolisio. [*Protectively.*] Let me think . . . I'll find a solution.

Reporter. [*To* Brandolisio.] You, a married man with children, aren't you ashamed to lead on this poor innocent girl? [*Ironically.*] A car, huh? A little house . . . Well, hurrah for our hide merchant.

Brandolisio. And what do you know about my life? What if I had a business that was much more important than just a leather factory? A very old firm, for example?

Ariadne. [*To the* Reporter.] Besides, I'm of age.

Brandolisio. [*To* Ariadne.] I've got it! I'll put you in the sales department of the "Narcissus" beauty salon. [*From this point on* Cosmo *will hang on every word of the dialogue, and his darkening face will alternate between scorn and despair.*]

Ariadne. [*Exultant.*] No more dusty rags, moth-eaten furs, worn-out things?

Brandolisio. [*Smiling.*] No more. You will be in charge of crystal vials, scented powders, tortoiseshell combs, leather cases, and silver boxes.

Reporter. [*To* Ariadne.] I'd be careful if I were you. [*Nods toward* Brandolisio.] He is just the type to be a white slaver.

Tanya. [*To the* Reporter.] Oh, really, what business is it of yours? It's easy to moralize. And this poor girl is supposed to rot here forever? For what? For your abstract morality? [*She puts an intimate and protective arm beneath* Ariadne's *arm.*]

Brandolisio. [*To* Tanya.] In the Ladies' Auxiliary, I'll have you named Patron of Orphaned Salesgirls.

Tanya. [*Beaming at* Ariadne.] And you will be my favorite ward. [*To* Brandolisio.] Don't worry, sir, I'll take care of everything.

Reporter. [*Slapping his thigh and doubling up from laughter.*] Ah, this is great! [*Aping* Tanya's *voice.*] Don't worry, sir, I'll take care of the little one. [*Returns to his former tone of voice.*] I would never have imagined that Ladies' Auxiliaries assumed such responsibilities.

Chanusky. [*Bitterly.*] Look, our poverty gives you no right to be insolent.

Reporter. [*Ill-humored.*] I don't have to give any explanations to a nobody like you.

Brandolisio. Mr. Chanusky is no longer a nobody. He is a D.P.N.P. First-Prize Winner . . . Take that down for your newspaper. I'll give you an exclusive for your "Man of the Hour" column. [*To* Chanusky.] Do you have a photograph?

Chanusky. [*Very emotional.*] No, sir, but that will be the first thing I'll do as soon as I get the prize money.

Brandolisio. At least five hundred copies. The tabloids will make you a celebrity. [*Slight pause.*] You might write under each photo: Tomorrow it could happen to you! [*He winks.*] A little publicity for me, too, don't you think?

Chanusky. [*Reeling from happiness.*] Sir, I . . . [*He pales and drops into a chair mumbling.*] Ho dog, pleh em ot raeb pu.

Tanya. [*Hurries to fan him.*] Peter, Peter, calm down. [*To* Brandolisio.] When he gets upset, he pronounces words backwards, "Ho dog" instead of "Oh God," and "Pleh em ot raeb pu" means "Help me to bear up." It is nothing serious, but you have to be careful because of the neurovegetative system . . . Then, too, his father had a hyperthyroid condition.

Brandolisio. [*Authoritatively.*] Don't be afraid, madam, it isn't his turn yet.

Cosmo. [*Taking a few steps toward* Ariadne.] Ariadne . . .

Ariadne. [*Gives a start as though waking from a dream.*] What is it?

Cosmo. [*After a moment of hestitation.*] Nothing! [*Returns to* Chalcedony *who looks at him sadly.*]

Ariadne. Cosmo, you must leave. You're just a boy. You don't understand what life is like. I loved you, I still love you, but you have to understand that . . .

Cosmo. [*With a hoarse shout.*] Stop! Don't say anything more! [Brandolisio *follows the scene carefully.*]

Ariadne. [*To* Chalcedony.] You've had more experience, you tell him.

154 *The Siege*

Chalcedony. [*Sadly.*] It wouldn't do any good . . . Everyone must learn grief all by himself.

Cosmo. [*To* Chalcedony *in a muted voice.*] Why didn't you leave me at the bottom of the mine? [Chalcedony *gets up and* Cosmo *runs into his brother's arms for a moment, but he suddenly withdraws as though ashamed of having shown weakness, and he turns his back on everyone.*]

Ariadne. [*Screaming.*] Cosmo . . . [*She stops with an expression of suffering on her face.*]

Brandolisio. [*To* Ariadne.] I'm sorry that I unwittingly . . .

Ariadne. No, sir, it is not your fault. It was I who shouldn't have . . . [*She covers her face with her hands for a moment, then continues in a sorrowful voice.*] A prisoner, do you see? A prisoner of my own flesh . . . And my soul flaps around like a meadowlark in a cage, a soul ensnared in the hope of flying up into the blue of the sky . . . But it can't. Its wings are weighted down with the mud of the whole world. Nobody's fault, really . . . [*Looks with tears in her eyes toward* Cosmo.] And his fault less than anyone's. [*To* Brandolisio *with sudden desperation.*] Do something for him . . . I'll give up everything, but save him . . . I know you can, I feel it. [*She stops, panting, and stares with wide eyes at* Brandolisio, *who has bowed his head; then as though seized by a premonition, she screams.*] Cosmo, Cosmo . . . [*She tries to run toward the boy, but* Brandolisio *grabs her by the arm and stops her.*]

Brandolisio. [*In a hard voice.*] You know very well that we are under siege . . . and you more than anyone else.

Ariadne. [*In a kind of hysterical crisis.*] I want nothing from you. Let me go! I have a right to be free, too.

Brandolisio. [*Coldly.*] And the past?

Ariadne. The past is mine, no one has the right . . . [*She stops, looks agonizingly toward* Cosmo.]

Brandolisio. I won't be the one to bring it up. It will come back all by itself. [*Nods toward the boy.*] And he knows it and fears it more than you do. He won't even turn around, for fear of reading the past in your face, your eyes, your mouth that still bears the imprint of other ardent lips . . . [*A heavy silence, then the telephone rings.*]

Reporter. [*Almost incredulously.*] The telephone . . . Don't you hear it? The telephone . . . [*He rushes to it and picks up the receiver.*] Hello . . . Hello.

Faraway Voice. [*Muffled but still quite intelligible.*] Long distance calling. Is this 77752?

Reporter. [*Excitedly.*] What? Just a moment . . . [*To* Isaac.] What's your number?

Brandolisio. [*Authoritatively taking the receiver from the* Reporter's *hand.*] Let go! It's for me.

Reporter. [*Angrily.*] Who told you it is for you?

Faraway Voice. Is Mr. Brandolisio there? A person-to-person call for Mr. Brandolisio from "Voices of the World." Go ahead!

[*Silence.* Brandolisio *looks into the eyes of the* Reporter *who, as though subdued, takes a few steps backward.* Brandolisio *has the receiver in his hand but he does not put it to his ear. One hears buzzing, mixed in with the connection and disconnection of telephone lines. Then, from everywhere, there begin to be heard isolated, broken sentences and bits of conversation, as happens when there is interference on the line. The heart-rending cries of babies, the anxious voices of women, the sad or pitiless voices of men. All the evil in the world is heard in bits and pieces, over the wire; it gurgles in the receiver that* Brandolisio *is holding in his hand, his absentminded gaze fixed on nothingness. Pronounced in various tones, the phrases follow one right after the other, almost superimposed on each other.*]

Child's Voice. Mama, Mama, come help me . . . Save me!

Man's Voice. He was shot at dawn . . . [*Then, a woman's scream.*]

Anguished Voice of a Man. You can't do this, you can't . . . I have four children . . . My babies.

Woman's Voice. Murderers! Murderers!

Monotonous Voice of a Man. In accordance with articles 362 to 375 of the Penal Code, you are sentenced to prison . . .

Angry Voice of a Woman. The letter. *You* wrote that letter, you bastard. [*Feverishly, amid the noises of a scuffle.*] Kill me, I don't care. I am tired, tired, do you understand? . . .

Muffled Voice of a Man. We have to get him to the hospital immediately.

Another Man's Voice. My money . . . give me back my money!

Tearful Voice of a Child. You're hurting me, why are you hurting me?

Woman's Voice. Doctor, Doctor . . . Save him! [Brandolisio *hangs up the receiver slowly, then walks toward the rear staircase as everyone steps aside. The wind roars, as though a storm were about to break. The wind dies down, and weak bugle calls are heard, along with dim military orders; the steps of marching soldiers fade away and out.*]

Reporter. [*Cocking his ear.*] They're leaving . . . Do you hear? They are lifting the siege!

Chanusky. We are free . . . Tanya, listen!

Tanya. They are going away! Peter, our life is beginning again.

Isaac. Hurry, Ariadne. We'll get the shop open.

Moko. The nightmare is over. We are awakening from a bad dream.

Chalcedony. [*Smiling.*] I smell the salt air of the sea. [*Imitating a boat whistle.*] The steamboat's leaving . . . [*Bursts out laughing as though mad.*]

Reporter. [*Waving his arms.*] The world is beckoning to us.

Chanusky. Hurry, Ariadne, lead us out.

Reporter. Ariadne, where is my typewriter case?

Moko. Where is my red jacket, Ariadne? . . . My barricade red jacket. [*The delirium is at its height, attracting the attention of the audience to that part of the stage where the characters are grouped. The thud of* Cosmo's *body, falling face down on the floor, makes everyone turn toward the corner where the boy had been. There is a moment of stupefied silence; then a woman's shrill scream.*]

Ariadne. [*Running toward the body.*] Cosmo! Cosmo! [*She kneels beside the body of the suicide, carefully turns him over, but suddenly withdraws her hands in horror.*] Blood . . . blood! [*Another frightened silence. The telephone has begun to ring again but no one thinks of lifting the receiver.* Chalcedony, *horrified, does not dare to withdraw the screwdriver protruding from* Cosmo's *chest.*]

Moko. [*Looking around, terrified; he screams.*] Who is crying?! [*No one answers. Still more anguished, he repeats.*] Don't you hear there is somebody crying?! [Isaac *falls on his knees and raises his thin arms to the heavens, where the light has become as red as the fires of hell, while the curtain slowly closes.*]

The End

The Parkbench

A Play in One Act

by
Ezio d'Errico

Translated by Louis Kibler

Characters

An Old Man
A Young Man
A Girl
Dyna
A Short Man
A Blind Man
A Streetwalker

A white-barked, gnarled tree dominates the scene; recently pruned, it raises its lopped branches toward a gray sky. A weather-beaten parkbench stands beneath the tree. Here and there are rusty, wrought-iron chairs, one of them upside down. In the background is a bleak escarpment; a winding path passes over it. At the bottom of the path, a cast iron pipe supports a wire trash can half filled with waste paper. One presumes that behind the embankment is an open space where children are playing, because periodically the singsong voices of children playing ring-around-a-rosy can be heard.

An Old Man who seems to be a plaster statue is sitting on one end of the bench. The rest of the bench is occupied by a Young Man in a light-colored raincoat. The Young Man is stretched out in a disorderly way, with one leg bent beneath him and an arm dangling; he is sleeping with his mouth half open, and, if a newspaper on the ground did not lead one to suppose that he has fallen asleep while reading, the Young Man might seem to be the corpse of a murder victim.

As the curtain opens, all is motionless and silent except for the singsong of the children. Then a young Girl wearing the thick-lensed eyeglasses of the nearsighted enters from the right. She is dressed with a somewhat awkward elegance. She is neither pretty nor ugly, and she has a resigned but also stubborn expression. The Girl comes forward slowly, looking about her with the diffident air of myopic people. In one hand she carries an umbrella, in the other a large woven handbag. She stops uncertainly, then spies the parkbench, walks up to it and scrutinizes the sleeping man. She must like what she sees, because after an absentminded glance at the statue of the Old Man, she goes to a chair, touches it, and realizes it is wet. She goes toward another chair and makes the same discovery. Finally she picks up the overturned one and, after making sure that it is dry, drags it over to within a yard of the bench, sits down, exchanges her eyeglasses for a different pair that she takes out of her handbag along with a book, and begins to read.

The children's singsong of ring-around-a-rosy ends in an outburst of shrill young voices. Jolted awake, the Young Man sits up facing the audience, yawns, picks up the newspaper, and with the surly air of someone who is not yet fully awake, rubs his arm, which has evidently gone to sleep.

Girl. [*Between her teeth.*] Finally.
    [*The Young Man throws her a sidelong glance.*]

Girl. Excuse me, but you know, when you sleep you are frightening. [*Smiling.*] Of course, it is not your fault.

Young Man. Frightening in what way?

Girl. I mean that your way of stretching out is a little macabre.

Young Man. No one was forcing you to look at me.

Girl. That's true; but parks are public places, and your apparent death seemed to fit in with the atmosphere. I couldn't help it.

[*The* Young Man *takes his time in answering and looks in all his pockets for his cigarettes.*]

Girl. [*Returns to her reading.*] Naturally I am happy for you and for everyone that you were only sleeping. The first warm days of spring do make one want to sleep.

[*The* Young Man, *who has finally found his cigarettes, looks up at the leaden sky.*]

Girl. [*Raising her eyes.*] Oh, of course . . . the sky isn't exactly blue, but the calendar can't be wrong. Today is March 21st, Saint Benedict's day . . . with the traditional saying about swallows and springtime.

Young Man. [*With a sneer.*] Are you waiting for the swallows? Do you feel like waiting for . . . [*makes the gesture of working a spray can.*] Pff . . . Pff . . .

Girl. What does that mean?

Young Man. Insecticides. No more insects and therefore no more swallows.

Girl. That's a shame. Especially for poets. [*Slight pause.*] But the scientists will invent something else.

Young Man. [*Who has lit the cigarette.*] Swallows made from synthetic fibers.

Girl. And why not? Even poets have to pay the price of progress and civilization. Anyway, you can't expect to have everything, swallows *and* computers.

Young Man. In any case, *you* are not looking for swallows.

Girl. No, I am looking for a husband.

Young Man. In parks?

Girl. Everywhere. I have divided the city into sectors. Today is my day to look in parks.

[*The* Young Man *smokes in silence.*]

Girl. Are you shocked?

Young Man. Not exactly.

Girl. Yet it's obvious that you are upset that a girl would declare openly that she is looking for a husband. [*Slight pause.*] It seems to me a very legitimate endeavor. First I get my diploma, then a nice job, and finally a husband. But don't get the idea that I think about it from morning to night. Only on Sundays. On other days I have my work, which is a source of great satisfaction to me.

Young Man. Mine is not.

Girl. Are you married?

Young Man. No, and I like it that way.

Girl. Don't fool youself. Contrary to popular belief, a woman can live by herself very well; a man cannot. A man needs somebody who will dust off his hopes and mend his inevitable depressions. [*Slight pause.*] And then, too, when children come along, what can a man do all by himself?

Young Man. If a man stays all by himself, children won't come along.

Girl. Naturally, but that is against the laws of nature and against the teachings of the Church. [*Slight pause.*] And I don't say that just because I have an uncle who is a bishop. [*Visibly bored, the* Young Man *looks off into space.*]

Girl. Don't think that my uncle is one of those surly and intolerant prelates. On the contrary. He is a very broad-minded man, and he has let me lead my life the way I see fit. He would have liked me to take a course in radio and television repairing, but when I told him that I really didn't feel cut out for that, all he did was spread his arms and mutter: "Better a good wife than a bad TV technician."

Young Man. [*After a while.*] Why don't you marry one of your co-workers?

Girl. Because they are all married. [*The* Young Man *makes a gesture of desperation.*]

Girl. But that doesn't matter. What were we talking about? Oh, yes, children. That's it. Whatever you may thing about them, you have to have children; they are the poetry of life.

[*From the other side of the embankment there is an outburst of children arguing; one voice, louder and more shrill than the others, emerges.*]

Child's Voice. [*Offstage.*] You sonsabitches! You bastards! Yes, bastards! [*Dyna comes running down the path, turning around every so often as though she is afraid of being followed. Some rocks, thrown from behind the escarpment, fall around her.*]

Dyna. [*Stops, panting.*] Bastards! [*She spits toward her invisible adversaries, then goes to sit on the bench between the* Old Man *who remains immobile and the* Young Man *who turns slightly to look at her. Dyna has the voice and the gestures of a five- or six-year-old child—but without ever being babyish; actually, she is an adolescent, small in stature but with a saucy body. She is poorly dressed, and her face is that of a retarded child; but her eyes are beautiful and her smile almost provocative.*]

Girl. [*To the* Young Man.] Do you have a job?

Young Man. What? Oh, yes, of course. [*Casts another sidelong glance at* Dyna.]

Girl. What business are you in?

Young Man. Banking.

[Dyna *suddenly begins to whistle "Garibaldi's Hymn," but stops after the first stanza like a bird that has exhausted its repertory. Then she turns to the* Old Man.]

Dyna. Pop . . . I'm hungry.

[*The* Old Man *takes a small, wrapped package from his pocket and silently hands it to* Dyna, *who unwraps it, takes out a small loaf of bread, and goes somewhat haughtily to throw the wrapper in the trash can. Then she returns to the bench, crouches like a monkey on the backrest, and begins to chew, but not without first throwing a smile to the* Young Man.]

Girl. As I was saying, my uncle is a very modern clergyman. And he also has a big heart. When I tell him I'm getting married, he will want to officiate at the ceremony. [*The* Young Man *continues to smoke in silence.*] Naturally, a marriage performed by a bishop would be very formal. I'll have to have a dress with a train. A rather long train . . . and the groom in morning dress. [*Slight pause.*] You wouldn't happen to own a frock coat, would you?

Young Man. No, and I wouldn't buy one even if they made me a cabinet member.

Girl. Do you think it is a useless expense? Why, you can always use a frock coat. Ceremonies, receptions, symposia, society parties . . . I'm sure the president of your bank has a frock coat. A somewhat old-fashioned one, perhaps. [Dyna *touches the shoulder of the* Young Man *and when he turns, she smiles at him.*] Anyway, I have planned my future. Marriage in a white dress with a train. A short honeymoon to Florence, Rome, and Naples. I am already a member of a condominium group and I have a right to a three-bedroom apartment, with bath and elevator, all payable in installments extending over a period of twenty-five years. I want at least two children, a boy and a girl. Public schools—but a good religious education. Frequent walks, a few visits to museums, some concerts, two weeks in the mountains in the summer . . . *Mens sana in corpore sano* . . . In this way one cares for one's biological patrimony, one makes a contribution to the formation of tomorrow's ruling class and . . . [Dyna *explodes with a resonant raspberry. The* Girl *stops talking. She puts her book and reading glasses in her handbag, puts on her other glasses, goes up to* Dyna *and very calmly slaps her face. The retarded girl drops her bread and bursts out with loud screams, throwing her mouth wide open like a cavern. The* Old Man *remains impassive.*]

Girl. [*To the* Young Man.] I hope to see you again under happier circumstances. [*She nods slightly with her head and struts off stage right. After the* Girl *has left,* Dyna *stops crying and smiles at the Young Man.*]

Young Man. [*To the* Old Man.] I'm sorry.

[*The* Old man *turns slowly to look at the* Young Man *as if he has only now become aware of his presence. Then he goes back to staring into space.*]

Young Man. . . . about what happened.

Old Man. [*Without moving.*] Don't worry about it. Dyna's used to it. Even when she plays with children all she does is give slaps and get them back.

Young Man. I assure you I hadn't expected that.

Old Man. Human reactions are often unpredictable.

Young Man. You are very understanding.

[Dyna, *visibly bored, gets down from the bench, starts up the path and halfway to the top sits down with her elbows on her knees and her chin resting in the palms of her hands, observing the two men from above.*]

Young Man. [*After a pause.*] Is she a relative of yours?

Old Man. She's my daughter.

Young Man. Oh . . . [*Slight pause.*] She's very young.

Old Man. She's fifteen.

Young Man. Fifteen? [*Pause.*] A . . . disease?

Old Man. No . . . She just stopped growing [*points a finger to his forehead*] up here. She stopped at five years.

Dyna. [*Shouting from her observation post.*] Hey! [*The* Young Man *turns and the retarded girl throws him a kiss with the tips of her fingers.*]

Young Man. Her development stopped when she was five? Poor thing.

Old Man. She doesn't suffer.

Young Man. Well, it's still a misfortune. For the family, I mean.

Old Man. I'm a widower.

Young Man. Oh . . . But for the girl, too.

Old Man. Nature is provident. It takes away the light, but it illuminates the darkness.

[*A silence.*]

Young Man. And what do the doctors say? Haven't they tried . . .

Old Man. Everything. Poisons, microbes, hormones, antibiotics, serums, electric treatments. A waste of time!

Young Man. Have you thought of institutionalizing her?

Old Man. Where? There is no room in the insane asylum. You need influence to get somebody in there. And then if I'm not around she starts breaking everything. She rebels, screams, bites, and they have to strap her down. [*Slight pause.*] I don't like them to strap her down. [*Another pause.*] But with me she is pretty good. She has her rags, her ribbons that she dresses up in . . . The worst she ever does is snitch little things that she hides and then forgets about. A few days ago my pistol disappeared. Who knows where she put it.

Young Man. A pistol?

Old Man. Oh, an old piece of junk from the days when I was in the service.

Young Man. Military service?

Old Man. No, night watchman. I took the job because I had insomnia. [*Slight pause.*] The pistol was part of the uniform, like the cap and the bicycle.

Young Man. And you made your rounds all night long?

Old Man. Sticking little stamps on the shutters of shops. But I was free during the day, so I could read. Reading has always been my passion.

Young Man. Oh . . . And what did you read?

Old Man. Books on anarchy, propaganda leaflets, nihilist newspapers. [*Slight pause.*] I am an anarchist.

Young Man. And at night you protected private property.

Old Man. I only stuck on the stamps. That's what they paid me for. [*Slight pause.*] Besides, I am a theorist. Naturally I don't disapprove of direct action, but violence is not my specialization. I like the idea of anarchy in an abstract way. People cannot understand the beauty of a utopia . . .

Young Man. Well, I have to admit that I, too . . .

Old Man. . . . cannot understand? That's because you have a brain. With a brain you can make calculations, conduct business, maybe even make scientific discoveries. But try listening to music with your brain. The same thing is true of a lot of other things.

Young Man. And you thought about those other things as you went about the city at night?

Old Man. Yes.

Young Man. [*Smiles.*] That's nice. [*As if to himself.*] Miles of streets, squares illuminated by the moon . . . or else fog and silence . . . Everyone is sleeping peacefully because there is an anarchist keeping watch.

Old Man. And waiting.

Young Man. For what?

Old Man. The bombs. And they came. I saw the city slowly destroyed. So I stuck the stamps on the ruins. [*Slight pause.*] After the bombings, the houses showed their medieval framework . . . Their true souls. [*Pause.*] At dawn I would tell these things to my girlfriend.

Young Man. The mother of the little girl?

Old Man. Yes. The only woman I ever loved. She was stone deaf, and I could talk to her without arguing and without the bitterness that comes from not being understood. I would talk, and she would smile at me sweetly. Those were happy days.

Young Man. Well, now that you're retired you can take it easy.

Old Man. Retired, yes, but I don't take it easy, because I think. [*Makes a horizontal gesture with his hands.*] When I'm dead I won't think any more, and then I'll take it easy. Finally.

Young Man. You may find this odd, but I can't believe that I will die.

Old Man. That's not odd. It's one of nature's little tricks. But without death, birth would have no sense. [*Slight pause.*] Even the world will die. I mean that it will be destroyed. Some very intelligent people are studying night and day to that end. I won't live to see it. But you may.

Young Man. Do you believe that nothing can be done to prevent it?

Old Man. I believe that nothing *should* be done to prevent it.

[Dyna *comes down the path and goes to sit between the* Old Man *and the* Young Man, *arranging herself in an ingenuous and worldly pose.*]

Young Man. [*After a glance at the retarded girl.*] It's as if . . . as if she lived outside.

Old Man. She does live outside. [*Slight pause.*] In her earthly paradise.

[*The* Young Man *involuntarily looks at the tree.* Dyna *crosses her legs and slowly lifts her skirt up to her groin, showing a thigh to the* Young Man. *Calmly, the* Old Man *pulls her clothing back down.*]

Young Man. [*Feigning indifference.*] Do you often take her to parks?

Old Man. Every day, when the weather is nice. [*Pause.*] It's a quiet place, there aren't many people about, and it's also convenient. [*Pointing with a finger.*] We live over there. [*Slight pause.*] Dyna has grown fond of this bench.

Young Man. [*Smiling.*] Dyna . . . That's a nice name. It's soft, musical.

Old Man. Yes. It's short for Dynamite.

Young Man. Ah!

Joyous Voices of Children. [*Offstage.*] Dyna . . . Dyna . . .
 [*The retarded girl stands up and goes running up the path until she disappears behind the barren escarpment.*]
Young Man. [*Who has followed her with his eyes.*] She's going to play.
Old Man. Yes. [*Pause.*] With children she plays. [*Another pause.*] With adults it is different. [*A silence.*] She doesn't realize . . . and some men take advantage of her. [*Pause.*] Almost always married men.
Young Man. And you haven't gone to the police?
Old Man. What's the use? [*Pause.*] And anyway you have to tell them everything, summon witnesses, call in a doctor for an examination . . . It's disgusting. [*Pause.*] For my daughter these things are very innocent, like eating or sleeping. It ought to be that way for others, too. [*Pause.*] Once it must have been . . . then, I don't know when and I don't know who, or based on what laws . . . Anyway they dirtied everything.
 [*The* Young Man *still gazes at the tree with its lopped-off branches jutting out to the leaden sky. A* Short Man *smoking a pipe enters from the left. He is dressed in a tattered sweater beneath a jacket that is too short, and he is wearing a bowler hat. His body is frail, his face sallow and wrinkled.*]
Short Man. [*Ceremoniously lifting his hat.*] Hello!
Old Man. How are you?
Short Man. Okay . . . [*Raising his eyes to the sky.*] When I was young, on Sundays there was always a little bit of sunshine for the poor.
 [*He sits down between the* Old Man *and the* Young Man.]
Old Man. Did you go to the C.R.A.N.I.C.?
Short Man. Yesterday.
Old Man. Good news?
Short Man. Who knows? They shout in the telephone, bells are ringing everywhere, people come and go banging the doors. It's a madhouse.
Old Man. [*To the* Young Man.] They have promised him a good job.
Young Man. In a firm?
Old Man. In an acronym: C.R.A.N.I.C. . . . cee, arr, a, en, i, cee.
Short Man. A very important acronym, with branches throughout the world and millions in assets . . . a whole string of zeroes.
Young Man. And what position are you to occupy in this acronym?
Short Man. [*Haughtily.*] Assistant porter. But with a uniform, because without the uniform, I won't accept.
Old Man. I wouldn't be so demanding. [*To the* Young Man.] What do you think?

Young Man. I don't know. It depends on what they give him to do.

Short Man. [*In a capricious tone.*] Assistant porter! A six-month trial period and then a permanent job.

Young Man. Fine. But what will your duties be?

Short Man. Who knows? It's a job I've never done before.

Young Man. Well, what does the porter do?

Short Man. [*With a sigh of forbearance.*] There isn't one.

Young Man. Then why are they hiring an assistant porter?

Short Man. So they can pay him less.

Old Man. [*In a conciliatory tone to the* Short Man.] At the end of two years, according to the union contract, they will have to promote you to porter. Two years pass quickly.

Short Man. [*Shrugging his shoulders.*] Ten years have already passed.

Old Man. Yeah, but that was a different matter.

Short Man. It's always the same matter. Nothing changes. But I want that uniform.

[*The* Old Man *spreads his arms in despair. A silence.* Dyna *reappears and comes skipping down the path; she goes and takes the chair that the nearsighted* Girl *had occupied, moves it close to the* Young Man, *and sits down, crossing her legs in the somewhat childish manner of a great lady.*]

Short Man. [*To the* Old Man.] How did she behave?

Old Man. Not badly. Today she has her eye on that young man.

Short Man. This one? What's so great about him?

Old Man. I don't know . . . she must have found him attractive.

[*The* Short Man *examines the* Young Man *as if to determine the extent of his fascination.*]

Young Man. [*A little uncomfortable, he rises.*] Well . . . I have to be going.

Old Man. No, please. Wait until she goes back to her playing.

Short Man. If you don't, she'll probably run after you and make a scene.

Old Man. [*To the* Young Man.] I'm sorry.

Young Man. [*Sitting back down.*] Well, all right.

Short Man. [*In a euphoric tone.*] Enjoy this nice bench. [*Slight pause.*] Is this the first time you have come here?

Young Man. It is.

Short Man. Then you really can't appreciate it.

Young Man. Well . . .

Short Man. No, no, let a man of experience explain. Parks are the islands of the city, and benches are their reefs. Every once in a while a new shipwrecked victim arrives. New in a manner of speaking, because in the long run we all know each other.

[*A tall young man, dressed with provincial elegance, enters from the right. His wavy hair is shiny with brilliantine, he has large dark glasses, and he walks leaning slightly backward and tapping the ground with a cane. When the* Blind Man *draws near to the bench,* Dyna, *afraid of getting hit with the cane, scurries away and goes to sit on the ground in front of the* Old Man, *facing the audience. The* Blind Man, *having determined that the seat is empty, sits down.* Dyna *observes him attentively, then she smiles at the* Young Man *as though to reassure him.*]

Blind Man. [*To the* Young Man.] Excuse me . . . Is there a woman nearby?

Young Man. What?

Blind Man. I asked if there is a woman around.

Young Man. No.

Blind Man. [*Sniffing the air.*] I must have been mistaken.

[*Offstage there is a joyful outcry. Shouts of "the balloon, the balloon!" are heard. Everyone except the* Blind Man *looks up and follows something—probably a balloon that has escaped from a child's hand—across the sky.*]

Old Man. [*To* Dyna, *giving her a coin.*] Here . . . go see if the balloon man is around.

[*With a little cry of joy,* Dyna *takes the coin, climbs up the path, and disappears.*]

Old Man. [*Rising.*] That's that. I'll go to meet her, and we'll leave by the other entrance. [*To the* Young Man.] Excuse me again. [*To the* Short Man.] Good luck with the uniform. [*He exits, stooped over, toward the rear.*]

Young Man. Good-bye.

Short Man. [*With a vague gesture.*] So long! [*Then he moves over on the bench to where the* Old Man *was sitting.*]

Short Man. [*To the* Young Man.] Move a little that way. [*To the* Blind Man.] There is room for you, too.

Young Man. [*Moving aside.*] I have to leave . . .

Short Man. Now where can you expect to find a more comfortable bench? [*He leans back and smokes with little puffs.*] And if the sun does not come here, we'll go to Methuselah's. Do you know Methuselah's bench?

Young Man. No.

Short Man. [*Indicating a distant point to the right.*] That one down there . . . There is always an old stray cat on it. A red cat, blind in one eye and bobtailed. They call him Methuselah. [*Gives a satisfied laugh.*] Cats are smart animals, pensive—and experts on the weather. Wherever a cat goes, sooner or later the sun will shine there.

Blind Man. [*To the* Young Man.] Was she a child?

Young Man. Who?

Blind Man. The one who went to buy a balloon.

Young Man. [*Snorting.*] Yes.

Blind Man. It is the first time that I have been wrong.

Young Man. [*To the* Short Man.] And before you were an aspiring assistant porter, what did you do?

Short Man. I was in prison. [*Slight pause.*] I used to make baskets. Baskets with no bottoms. For ten years I wove baskets with no bottoms.

Young Man. Ten years?

Short Man. They went very fast.

Young Man. And always weaving baskets?'

Short Man. Without bottoms. It's interesting work. Do you know how a wicker basket is woven?

Young Man. Only vaguely.

Short Man. There are various ways. Herringbone weave, plaited, vertical weave. I became very good at it. My baskets were the best. [*He illustrates with gestures.*] Wide at the mouth and then puffed out, and becoming increasingly narrow, like the thighs of a woman. The warden was very pleased with me and pointed me out as an example. But I tried to go too far. That is where I went wrong. I wanted the basket to have a bottom. But the head guard had it in for me, and he read off an ancient regulation that makes no provision for basket bottoms.

Young Man. And why not?

Short Man. I don't know. You can't argue with regulations.

Young Man. But what good is a basket with no bottom?

Short Man. To keep the inmate occupied. [*Slight pause.*] To give me a little satisfaction, the warden sent a report to the Bureau of Penal Institutions, telling them about an inmate who wanted to make bottoms for the baskets. The reply was that regulations could not be broken. When the warden read me the letter, the head guard rubbed his hands together and said that it served me right and that I was a subversive. Then I called him a stupid jackass. He kicked me, and I stuck one of the baskets over his head. [*Slight pause.*] Two more years.

Young Man. What?

Short Man. They tried me, and I got two more years for insubordination and assault. The lawyer pointed out that there were extenuating circumstances, that I had been provoked, but since I was a habitual criminal . . .

Young Man. Ah, because you had already . . .

Short Man. It's a long story. I got my first conviction when I was a soldier. A year in prison for having sold two cans of government-issued meat. I don't like canned meat, and I wanted to buy some sardines. Then, because of brawls with the guards, I continued to accumulate convictions, and instead of one year I did ten.

Blind Man. Excuse me for interrupting. You spent ten years in prison?

Short Man. To be exact, nine years, ten months, and fourteen days.

Blind Man. And how old are you?

Short Man. I'm thirty-two now.

Blind Man. And for nine years, ten months, and fourteen days, the only feminine thighs that you ever got your hands on were those of baskets?

Short Man. Naturally. What's so odd about that?

Blind Man. Nothing, really, but . . . when you got out and found yourself with a real woman . . .

Short Man. Ah, . . . well, the first time it wasn't easy . . . Then, I thought up a gimmick. All I had to do was think of a basket. [*He laughs.*]

Voice of the Old Man. [*Offstage.*] Dyna! Come here! Dyna! [*Dyna, with the string of a red balloon tied to her waist, comes dashing down the path. She goes up to the* Young Man, *plants a kiss on his mouth, then runs away while the angry cries of the* Old Man *can still be heard.*]

Blind Man. Was that a child, too?

Young Man. [*Between his teeth.*] Yes.

Blind Man. Excuse me.

Young Man. [*To the* Short Man.] Anyway, now you are free.

Short Man. So what?

Young Man. I mean . . . well, you can do what you want. You can even make basket bottoms.

Short Man. Yes, that's true . . . I would have liked to have got work like that. But now they make baskets by machine, out of plastic. [*Slight pause.*] I should never talk about these things. They make me sad.

Young Man. I'm sorry, I didn't mean . . .

Short Man. No, it's not your fault. Even when I am alone I think about it, and at night I dream about baskets.

Blind Man. [*As though to himself.*] I dream about women.

Short Man. [*Brightening and pointing at something to the right.*] Look!

Young Man. What is it?

Short Man. [*Rising.*] A ray of sun on Methuselah's bench. We have to take advantage of it. If you'll excuse me . . . [*He exits excitedly to the right, turning around every so often and indicating that it is indeed a ray of sunshine, until he disappears. Silence.*]

Blind Man. [*In a confidential tone.*] Now you can tell me . . . That person who came to give you a kiss, was she a woman?

Young Man. [*With a sigh.*] Okay, it was a woman.

Blind Man. Young?

Young Man. Very young.

Blind Man. [*Satisfied.*] I've never been mistaken.

Young Man. You can sense them with your nose?

Blind Man. I can sense them in every way.

Young Man. And you can never have them.

Blind Man. Me? I can have as many as I want. At the moment I have a steady and then, when lady luck smiles . . .

Young Man. Ah, . . . a steady girl?

Blind Man. [*Smiling.*] Yes, she's sleeping now. [*Very seriously.*] In fact, I left the house just to let her rest. She has a right to it. She works all night.

Young Man. What kind of work?

Blind Man. How old are you?

Young Man. Old enough.

Blind Man. And you don't understand?

Young Man. Ah . . .

Blind Man. [*With a sigh.*] But you can't live by bread alone. That's why I fantasize, dream . . . How can you help it? Everyone is made differently. And women feel an attraction toward a certain kind of man.

Young Man. I see. [*Pause.*] And while your steady sleeps, you . . .

Blind Man. I watch her place.

Young Man. What place?

Blind Man. This bench. It's very much in demand, you know. There are no street lights within two hundred yards.

Young Man. [*Glancing around.*] You're right.

Blind Man. You have to watch the competition. And this is the most dangerous time of day. Toward evening the women who don't have a regular place start arriving and they want to take over the bench. [*He makes a face.*] Two-bit whores, even old ones who ought to be retired.

[*From the right appears the* Girl *with the eyeglasses and the woven handbag. Somewhat undecided, she stops.*]

Blind Man. [*Startled.*] It's a woman!

Young Man. [*Turning around.*] Don't worry. I know her.

Girl. Am I interrupting?

Blind Man. [*To the* Young Man.] Ah, she's your date? [*Getting up.*] I'll leave.

Young Man. You can stay.

Blind Man. Really, now. I am a gentleman. [*To the* Girl.] Please sit down, miss. [*To the* Young Man.] Good-bye . . . [*He goes off to the left, tapping the ground with his cane.*]

Girl. [*Coming forward.*] Did I come at a bad time?

Young Man. [*Lighting a cigarette.*] Not at all.

Girl. [*Going to sit on the bench.*] I'm sorry I interrupted your conversation. [*Pause.*] Have you been talking to that blind man ever since I left?

Young Man. No, earlier there was a basket maker. Do you know how baskets are woven?

Girl. No.

Young Man. And you don't want to know. That's bad. There are so many things in the world that we do not have the slightest idea about. Then one fine day, on a reef . . . excuse me, on a parkbench, some monsters meet. [*He smiles.*] I'm not talking about deformed creatures . . . "Monster" comes from the Latin "monstrum," any unusual occurrence that shows the will of the gods. [*Slight pause.*] I said the monsters meet, but perhaps we have been living together forever, without knowing it.

Girl. Just a minute . . .

Young Man. [*As if to himself.*] Perhaps each of us, in his own way, is a monster. And doesn't know it.

Girl. I don't understand . . .

Young Man. I understood it only today . . . And yet everything has its reason for being. Every event, even the smallest one, meshes like a cogwheel with other events, and all together they form a machine that at a certain point can grab us and crush us. [*Slight pause.*] You still don't understand, do you?

Girl. [*Somewhat embarrassed.*] The fact is that the manufacture of baskets . . .

Young Man. With no bottoms.

Girl. With no bottoms, if you wish.

Young Man. Does not interest you. Okay. Let's say no more about it. And you are also not interested in blind men who are kept by streetwalkers, because they were born in a certain way that makes women go crazy, nor are you interested in cans of meat that send a man to prison for ten years, nor in Dyna and her earthly paradise . . . I won't go on.

Girl. [*A little frightened.*] Sir!

Young Man. Then let's talk about your wedding. A white dress with a train, let's say two yards, three yards, five yards long. Are five yards enough? Honeymoon. Florence-Rome-Naples. An apartment in the condominium association, a baby boy, a baby girl, et cetera. In a word . . . the Dark Ages! [*With a gesture he prevents the* Girl *from interrupting him.*] I have not finished. [*Smiling.*] Let's suppose that your husband is employed in a bank. For years he will continue to write down long columns of figures, putting up with his manager who owns a frock coat but who is peskier than a horsefly. Then he will become the manager, and he will entrust the surveillance of the bank to a night watchman who may be an individualistic anarchist. Do you think that anything will change? No . . . it is still the Dark Ages.

Girl. Please.

Young Man. Be patient just a little longer. Your children will go to school and will learn the same dumb things that we learned. Then they will go off to war singing, to get themselves gutted by strangers who will also be singing. Your uncle the bishop will bless both sides until someone will drop enough atomic bombs to reduce the earth to a ball of ashes, and only then will the Dark Ages be finished once and for all.

Girl. [*Gets up.*] Well, I never.

Young Man. So the night watchman is right. We mustn't try to prevent it. On the other hand, we can't change, because the Dark Ages are stronger than we are. We work in acronyms, where everyone shouts and the telephones jangle, each of us speaks an incomprehensible language, a bench is defended like a fortress, the sides of a basket become as exciting as a woman's thighs, you don't feel suited for radio-TV repair work, and Methuselah warms himself in the sun.

[*The* Girl, *after backing away terrified, lets out a little shriek and runs off to the left. The* Young Man *throws away his cigarette butt and puts his head in his hands. The reddish tones of sunset begin to tint the leaden sky until it seems to be a red hot lid.*

Dyna *enters from the left; she no longer has the balloon tied to her wrist, but she has wrapped a pink ribbon around her forehead and has pinned two strips of white tulle to her shoulders. She takes the ends of the tulle strips and lifts them so that they seem like wings; then lifting a foot, she strikes a pose as though she were about to take flight. From afar, perhaps from one of the houses scattered around the edge of the park, are heard the muffled notes of a piano. It is a Nocturne by Chopin. The director should pace the dialogue according to the crescendos and the pianissimos, so the background music will make it even more fantastic.*]

Dyna. [*Softly.*] Hey . . .
Young Man. [*Raising his head and smiling.*] Hey . . . [*With a short sprint,* Dyna *reaches the bench and goes to perch on the backrest.*] Where in the world did you come from?
Dyna. Ssssh . . . [*Smiles.*]
Young Man. And still outside? At this hour . . .
Dyna. If I want to, I'll stay out until yesterday.
    [*The* Young Man *does not reply.*]
Dyna. And I can come and go when and where I wish.
Young Man. What about your father?
Dyna. Quiet! Don't ever talk with the others.
Young Man. [*After a pause he looks at* Dyna *with smiling curiosity.*] Okay, but your father is mad at you. [*Dyna wrinkles her brow with an inquisitive expression.*]
Young Man. [*Still in the tone with which one speaks to a child.*] Where did you hide the pistol?
Dyna. What pistol?
Young Man. Okay, okay. Now don't pretend that you don't know what I am talking about. Your father's pistol. [*With his hand he makes the gesture of squeezing a trigger.*] Where did you put it?
Dyna. [*Looking around absently.*] The pistol is sleeping . . . It is sleeping and dreaming. [*In a deep voice.*] Boom . . . Boom . . . That's what pistols dream about. [*She laughs. The* Young Man *is silent as though afraid of disturbing the mystery of a being who lives perhaps in another dimension.*]
Dyna. The ones on the outside are crying. [*Smiling.*] Do you want to stand still with me?
Young Man. What do you mean, "stand still"?
Dyna. Many years ago.
Young Man. [*As though to himself.*] Stand still in the earthly paradise . . . [*Shakes his head.*] I don't deserve it.
Dyna. [*She shakes her hands slightly, then with a little cry she cups them together and opens them slowly before the eyes of the* Young Man.] Did you see?
Young Man. See what?
Dyna. Cheep . . . Cheep.
Young Man. [*Smiling.*] Are you pretending that your hands are a nest?
Dyna. [*Shrugs her shoulders, then takes one of the* Young Man's *hands.*] Why don't you touch me?
Young Man. [*Embarrassed, he withdraws his hand.*] Because . . . because it isn't right.
Dyna. Who said so?

Young Man. Well . . . I don't know . . . I really don't know who said
    so.
Dyna. [*In an amused and sad tone, in rhythm to the piano.*] Tim . . .
    Tam . . . Toom . . .
Young Man. [*Slowly staring off into space.*] And yet I am sure that
    someone said so . . . but I don't know who.
Dyna. A hundred years from now.
Young Man. That's it, very good . . . A hundred years from now.
Dyna. [*Suddenly changing her tone.*] Have you ever seen dead peo-
    ple? I have seen them.
Young Man. Where?
Dyna. [*With a gesture of plunging from top to bottom.*] Shooom! Down
    into the courtyard. [*Leaning forward from the backrest of the bench
    as though the dead woman were in front of the bench.*] Her naked
    body was all white and her eyes were big and black . . .
Young Man. Who was she?
Dyna. I don't know. She always went around in a nightgown.
    Always singing. [*Same gesture.*] Shooom!
Young Man. Don't think of dead people.
Dyna. [*With one of her habitual changes of mood, she takes the pink ribbon
    from her forehead and gives it to the* Young Man.] Here . . .
Young Man. [*Taking the ribbon.*] A gift?
Dyna. No.
Young Man. [*Smiling.*] A souvenir?
Dyna. No.
Young Man. Then . . . You're trying to tell me . . .
Dyna. Yes.
    [*The* Young Man *lowers his head, slowly folds the ribbon, and puts it in
    a pocket of his raincoat.*]
Young Man. [*Gently.*] Now you must go home.
Dyna. Why?
Young Man. Because it is late.
Dyna. Who are you waiting for?
Young Man. No one.
    [Dyna *laughs incredulously.*]
Young Man. I swear to you that I am not waiting for anyone.
Dyna. I swear to you . . . [*Laughs softly.*]
Young Man. Do you know what an oath is? It is a solemn promise.
    If I don't keep it, woe is me . . . [*Smiles.*]
Dyna. Yes. [*She turns to the right as though listening for something. The
    sound of the piano stops. Dyna nods her head as though imposing
    silence and climbs down from the bench.*]
Voice of the Old Man, Offstage. Dyna . . . Dyna! [Dyna *quickly kisses*

the Young Man, *then runs toward the path. She stops again for an instant, gives a childish gesture of farewell, then disappears.*]
Voice of the Old Man, Nearer. Dyna . . .
[*The* Young Man *gets up and remains staring at the place where* Dyna *disappeared. A* Streetwalker *enters from the left. She is rather old with a wrinkled face made grotesque by her makeup. The woman seems worried and turns as though she is afraid of being followed.*]
Streetwalker. [*Going to sit on the bench.*] May I sit down?
[*The* Young Man *turns to look at the last monster of his life.*]
Streetwalker. [*With a humble smile.*] Am I disturbing you? [*Then, when the* Young Man *turns his back on her and starts away . . .*] Listen . . . I'm sorry. [*The* Young Man *stops and turns around.*] Stay just a minute. [*Looking fearfully to the left.*] She might show up at any moment. [*Taking a cigarette from her purse.*] Pretend like you're giving me a light.
Young Man. [*Holding out his lit cigarette lighter.*] I'm sorry, but I'm in a hurry.
Streetwalker. Thanks . . . I'm only asking you to stay for a minute. Please . . . [*Looks again toward the left.*]
Young Man. What are you afraid of?
Streetwalker. [*Still looking toward the left.*] She's stopped . . . did you see? Sit down a moment.
Young Man. [*Sitting down on the bench.*] Who are you talking about?
Streetwalker. [*Still throwing suspicious glances into the darkening twilight.*] Carla . . . She thinks she's scaring me . . . [*Between her teeth.*] Her and her filthy blind man . . . [*In a doleful voice.*] I'm not young any more, I know that, but I have to eat, too . . . Even if no one sticks up for me. They are trying to bully me, don't you see?
Young Man. [*Somewhat annoyed, he tries to rise.*] Look, I . . .
Streetwalker. [*Hanging on to the* Young Man's *arm.*] Just a little longer . . . [*Keeps looking to the left.* Dyna *reappears at the top of the path. She stops and looks at the couple, then comes down quickly and silently.*]
Young Man [*Trying to free himself.*] Couldn't you go sit on another bench?
Streetwalker. [*Angrily.*] Why should I? Is Carla's name written on this bench? I used to come here before she did!
[Dyna *has put her arm into the trash can and draws out an old revolver. A shot is heard. Without a cry, the* Young Man *slumps on his side. The* Streetwalker *jumps to her feet with a muffled scream, then staggers back terrified and runs off to the right. In the confusion* Dyna *has quickly disappeared to the other side of the escarpment.*]

The dead man, lying on his back on the bench, is in the same position as at the beginning of the act, one leg bent under him and an arm dangling.

The sound of the piano begins again in the distance, with Chopin's Nocturne.

The nearsighted Girl *with glasses enters from the left. She leans toward the bench, draws near, and sits in the chair. She looks up, holds out her hand, and feels the first drops of rain, then opens her umbrella.*]

Girl. [*Timidly touching one of the* Young Man's *shoulders.*] Hey, it's raining, you know . . . [*With a slight smile.*] Now you're doing it on purpose. [*In a somewhat childish manner.*] You know you're a naughty boy? [*With a sigh.*] Okay, maybe I was wrong . . . But don't get it into your head that I am discouraged. [*Somewhat sadly.*] I'm used to being very patient. Otherwise, what would I do? [*Smiling.*] And then, too, I've thought it over . . . We can do without the train and the frock coat . . . [*Slight pause.*] When you get to know me better, you'll see that I'm a nice girl. [*She crosses her legs and pulls her skirt up a bit.*] I know that today men aren't satisfied with just moral qualities. [*Another little jerk to the skirt brings it up above her knees.*] And that's okay . . . just as long as you . . . just as long as you don't go too far . . .

The curtain slowly closes.

Index